# Contents

# ACKNOWLEDGEMENTS

What started off as an attempt to assimilate a story for the Rouse family soon turned into a larger project for wider circulation, and with that came the responsibility to research the context and check various facts.

I am indebted to a number of individuals and organisations who have helped me draw together information from sources beyond the family archive, particularly to those who have come up with specific records and allowed me to include them in this account.

I would particularly like to express gratitude to the following people: Charles Foster, author of *The Complete Dambusters*, who runs the Dambusters blog (and is the nephew of pilot David Maltby), Nick Bird, Director of Thorpe Camp Preservation Group at Woodhall Spa, Dave Gilbert at the International Bomber Command Centre, family members Simon Plumpton and Angela Fletcher, and my friend and former colleague Andrew Fisher.

Most of the illustrations used in this book are from the family collection, but some originate from external sources, and a list of these is given at the back, before the Appendices. Non-pictorial information sources are acknowledged at the point of use, in footnotes or Appendices.

I am especially grateful to my wife Amanda Williams and daughter Beth Bearman for the advice and practical assistance given to me in the preparation of this book. It goes without saying that any remaining errors or inadvertent omissions are entirely my responsibility, and I would intend to put such things right in any future edition.

Matthew Williams
September 2020

# FROM LEISTON TO
# LANCASTERS

## Harold Rouse's story

Edited by Matthew Williams

© Matthew Williams

First published in 2020 by Independent Publishing Network.

Distributed by SCT Books, 75 Christchurch Road, Norwich NR2 3NG.
info@smartcycletraining.co.uk

ISBN 978-1-83853-648-0


Typset in MS Calibri and Times New Roman by SCT Books

Manufactured in the UK by Imprint Digital, Exeter

*Front cover central image:  Extract from an original monochrome photograph, coloured by hand, Harold Rouse (centre) in January 1942 with fellow 97 Squadron crew members (clockwise from left): Max Smith, George Lancey, David Maltby (family collection).*

# INTRODUCTION

I first met Harold Clifford Rouse in the summer of 1975.

I was in the potentially disadvantageous position of being the schoolboy who had become the boyfriend of his beloved daughter Mandy (Amanda). I succeeded in embarrassing him in public in a restaurant quite early on, by not knowing that tartare sauce was meant for accompanying scampi, rather than being shovelled onto my steak.

Yet he was unfailingly understanding and courteous to this buffoon and potential young suitor. He allowed me to come along with him while taking or collecting Amanda from university - made possible because my college had slightly shorter terms than hers. And so, sitting beside him in the car on the outward or return journey, I got to know him better, and vice versa. Not only did he teach me the finer aspects of lunchtime condiments, but eventually even allowed me occasionally to take the wheel of his new car, by way of helping me learn to drive.

At no point during those months, nor indeed during the following two or three decades, do I recall him making more than passing reference to his experiences in the RAF during the Second World War. And there were plenty of opportunities he could have taken for re-living those memories during lively family gatherings - I shared in a few of those, because my relationship with Amanda survived three years at separate universities, and I went on to become his son-in-law.

If anything, I got to learn rather more about Harold's status as the Company Secretary of Blakes, a respected holiday firm based in the

Norfolk Broads, and his work in the local branch of the professional organisation looking after company accountants - the Institute of Cost & Management Accountants*. He organised the Institute's twice-yearly examinations held at the Assembly House in Norwich, where he was a well-known and popular figure. After he retired, he was asked to go back into work at Blakes for a time, and he was also in demand for his knowledge about the exams.

In the last few years of his retired life, and especially after he was widowed, he did become more forthcoming about that earlier part of his career, and in particular his wartime service. There was evidently a deep latent pride in having been part of 97 Squadron. This may have emerged because, by then, there was the opportunity to view many websites covering the activities of Bomber Command. Harold, who had bought himself a laptop, did not consider himself too old in his eighties to learn how to do that. Aside from his own impressive war record, it turned out that he was a key member of the first Lancaster aircrew skippered by David Maltby - a pilot who went on to become famous for his role in the 617 Squadron Dambusters mission.

It was in those last years that we realised there was a duty to later generations to at least record Harold's life experiences, not just in the RAF but in the time before that, growing up amongst a family in which he was the youngest sibling. We suggested to him that he might set down some reminiscences onto tape in conversation with Amanda. After a little persuasion and preparation, opportunities to do this were taken during intermittent home visits over a couple of years from around 2009. Thankfully, initial inhibitions about speaking into a Dictaphone rapidly evaporated, and he was soon talking freely, especially about his close family, with an extraordinary recall for

---

* Now known as the Chartered Institute of Management Accountants (CIMA)

specific dates and days of the week. The output was a series of digital recordings of stories under various themes, and not always in strict chronological order!

Hearing of his aircrew flight into Berlin in 1945 (this was eighteen months before the start of the famous airlift) led us to suggest that he might like to accompany us to that city. Our son was studying there and would welcome the opportunity of showing his Grandad around. And so he made that trip in 2012 at the age of 91, and a trickle of memories came out (after two-thirds of a century) that had not even found their way onto the tape.

*Harold in Berlin, November 2012, with his daughter and son-in-law*

After Harold's death in 2014 at the age of 92, the original recordings made by Amanda sat on my computer waiting to be turned into a written transcript. During the Coronavirus lockdown in 2020, there was at last the time to start the painstaking job of transcribing. It was a process of discovery about his interesting and varied early life.

Unpacking the story has, of course, been enhanced by the informative power of the internet, but also by reference to documents he had kept - not least his priceless RAF log book and a box of family photographs. He did not have these to hand during the original recordings, and most of the photos are unlabelled, but I have included selected pictures here as best I can to support the transcribed text. I have also placed some reference maps and lists in seven appendices towards the back of this book, followed by an index.

One of the themes that comes through in Harold's story is the talent he possessed in regard to both self-improvement and in helping others to progress. While his RAF career was dominated by the series of dangerous flying operations made in Lancasters between January and December 1942, he had been under training for much of the time before that, and the three years afterwards were essentially spent training others. Further on, he must have assisted countless accountancy trainees and exam candidates during his subsequent career. Lending his new car to help a nineteen-year-old develop some driving skills was only natural.

A second factor that stands out from the start of the story is the remarkably positive spirit of Harold's family: this was displayed equally by him and his brothers and sisters. It is noticeable that a good chunk of the narrative he wanted to share covered the years prior to World War Two, during the formative time he spent growing up in the Suffolk town of Leiston. All families have disappointments and tragedies, and his was no exception, yet Harold and his four older siblings seem to have been imbued with an unquenchably optimistic outlook and an open-minded interest in everything, and that carried on throughout their lives. For the four who escaped the tuberculosis that cruelly took Louie, this trait was associated with a longevity that cannot have been a coincidence.

Harold's mother and father, who came from a humble background, must have possessed a special knack for good parenting, and they were surely proud to see their son grow up to be the man he was.

Here is his story, told mostly in his own words.

# PART I: An upbringing

## Early days

Well, I was born on 12th April 1921 at number 19B Haylings Road, Leiston in Suffolk.[*] Dad had taken the time off from work, so he was at home and there was a maternity nurse, or whatever they called them in those days, in with Mum and me.

I'm told that my big sister Connie[†] and her friend Edie came out of school in the afternoon and walked up the road to our house, and Connie looked up at the bedroom window and saw a nurse walk across the window. 'Oh dear,' she thought, 'there's a nurse in there with my mum.'

So she went indoors, and Dad said to her, 'Well yes, you've got a little brother, and if you wait a minute, I'll see if you can go up and have a look at him.' Evidently, they did - I didn't know anything about it of course - and that's when Edie and Connie first saw me.

*Harold at about a year old, dressed in a style which was not unusual in those days*

As a youngster, I was often called by my middle name Cliff, rather than Harold. When Connie had left school - she was 13 on the 17th April and I was born on the 12th, she left school a year later - she eventually got a job with Mr and Mrs Powell, who ran the White Horse Hotel, and they lived over the top of the hotel down there. I'll mention

---

[*] This is now number 23 Haylings Road. See the map in Appendix 3
[†] See the family tree in Appendix 1

*The White Horse Hotel at the junction of Station Road and Main Street, Leiston, pictured in 2020*

them again later. Connie got a job as, I don't know, a maid or whatever, not in the hotel part, but in the living quarters with Mr and Mrs Powell.

Mum used to always do Mrs Powell's washing for her - her laundry. And I remember, I used to help her. I couldn't have been very old - about four years old, I don't think I'd started school – but Mum allowed me to go down the road to the White Horse with a little attaché case with Connie's clean clothes. It must have been on the Friday in the week, I should think. Of course, in those days there wasn't a lot of traffic on the roads, not motorised traffic, so it was quite safe really. I don't think Mother would have let me go down if there had been any danger.

And that's how I first came to know Mr Powell, who played a little part in our life later on - because he owned the house we got to rent after the war (I'm jumping about a bit, sorry!).

## Starting school (September 1926)

*Harold at between four and five years old, New Year 1926*

I got to the age of five and I started at the primary school at the bottom of the Saxmundham Road (I think it's actually called Waterloo Avenue), nearly opposite the White Horse Hotel.

And I remember my first teacher was a Miss Whiting. We weren't in a classroom - we were at the end of the hall, the assembly hall, and there were about twenty of us I suppose, something like that.

I can't remember much about what went on - obviously we were taught the alphabet, numbers and that sort of thing, and we did a bit of writing or scribbling. I slowly progressed through the school as I got older, and ended up, when I was ten, in the top class that they ran in the primary school, under Mrs Osborne. She was a very good teacher, a very nice teacher indeed.

We were a mixed class, girls and boys, and it was in there that we took our examination which would be called the eleven plus these days, but it didn't have any particular name then - just an

*A glimpse of Harold and his mother, front of 19B Haylings Road (now number 23), 1927*

*Northward aerial view of the centre of Leiston in 1920, showing the main works at Garrett's, also Haylings Road (left), and Central Road (right). This can be compared with the map in Appendix 3. The first three houses in which Harold lived are visible.*

examination. We were told if we did well, we stood a chance of going to the secondary school just up the road[*]. If not, we would be going to the senior school, which was next door to the secondary school, and take our further education from there.

And then I think it was the following week when we heard the results from the examination, and none of us had got a place in the secondary school - in fact, that year I don't think any Leiston pupil got a place at the secondary school. I think there was one from Aldeburgh who got it - I remember that his name was Dennis Mann. I didn't

---

[*] Leiston Grammar School

know at the time, but my dad had saved up money when he was at work, hoping to send me there - because they took private pupils as well as others. But evidently with the slump that came about at that time, he had to use it and it all went - though by the time that I was 11, which would be in 1932, I think Dad had got a job up in London which slowly put him back on his feet - but not enough to... well, what I didn't have I didn't miss, I'll put it that way. I do know a lot of the ones at the primary school - boys and girls - their parents were able to pay for them to go.

I went up to the senior school. In going up there were four of us, all boys, and we'd each done quite well in our work at the primary school, so we jumped a year up at the senior school. We went into Mr Clark's class. We spent eighteen months there before going on to the senior class, and had the last eighteen months with Mr Newbury.

I mustn't boast, but I did quite well at the senior school, and they seemed to look upon me as the top boy for some unknown reason. I played football for them, I played cricket for them, and I thoroughly

*Work in the foundry: Harold's father is pictured standing on the mould centre-right, helping to pour molten metal, late 1920s or early 1930s*

*The Rouse family in 1932: from left, back row, Louie, Bertie, Connie, Ernie.*
*Harold is in the middle behind seated Dad and Mum. Insert, school picture*
*taken in September 1932*

enjoyed my three years at the school. In the last year I was there, which was a girls' and boys' school, in the two top classes of the school, the boys were on their own and the girls were on their own. The other classes beneath us, they had the girls and boys in together.

The mistress who took over our class decided to form a dance group for country dancing. And I got chosen with Joyce Turner as my partner, to be the lead couple - there were eight pairs of us, I think. We did a number of country dances. I suppose the dances had names, but I just can't remember that - but I do remember how one of them went, the eight of us paraded, danced, came back, and the top two, Joyce and myself, she went one way, I went the other and got onto the tail end, and slowly we circulated like that.

We had a radiogram up there which we used to dance to, and we were getting ready to celebrate the 1935 celebrations for King George V and Queen Mary. And we were going to do an exhibition in the

LWAA* grounds up Victory Road. I remember I actually got in a bit of trouble after the last rehearsal before the event, after I had been asked to help with getting the radiogram back into the school. The girls helped me carry it and we put it on the front lawn by the front door. It was a lovely day. So we thought, we'll have a little rest. We sat down on the grass and had a laugh and a talk and so forth, and suddenly the headmaster Mr Clegg came round. I was marched back in and made to sit in the girls' class instead of my own (Mr Newbury's), given a blank piece of paper and told to write a composition on 'The Bluebell Wood'. In the event, I never managed to write a single word, but the girls' teacher let me off on that occasion.

On the day of the celebrations up at the LWAA, it seemed to go all right. The boys had to be dressed all in white - white shorts and white shirts and so forth - how Mother found the money to get me the shorts I don't know - and white socks and white plimsolls. And the girls were dressed in white dresses and white sashes and things like that. Anyway, it went quite well, so that was that.

That was just about my last day, as I thought, at school - I was fourteen then. I remember the Friday of that week, thinking to myself, well, it's the last day of school...

**Beginning work** (June 1935)

On the following Monday I started with Mr Burrage in his shop. He had a radio shop down Sizewell Road, but before I actually joined him, he'd moved into the High Street, just around the corner from, well right opposite, the Black Horse Hotel in the High Street. I spent a year after school doing that.

It was a combined shop - a radio shop selling wireless sets and big radiograms, things like that, toys, stationery and other similar goods. After he had moved, he'd taken on more merchandise to sell.

---

* Leiston Works Athletic Association

11

*Studio portrait photo taken around 1935*

At the back of the shop was a big shed. In those days, people had battery wirelesses. One of the batteries was a small one with a glass case and a handle on, and that was the starting machine of the radio - the accumulator they called them. On a Monday people used to bring their accumulators in to us, they'd got their names on the top, and my job was to take them into the shed at the bottom of the shop, clean up the terminals to get the rust off, load them up in banks of three (there would be 40 or 50 of these accumulators), connect them up to the wires inside there, and switch it on to charge up the batteries. And they were on charge until about the Friday of the week, when people came back in to pick up their accumulators ready for their weekend listening. Their names were meant to be on the top, so I knew whose were whose.

On top of that, Mr Burrage was also an agent for dry cleaning, which was done at a place in Ipswich actually, so we collected the clothes in the shop and sent them off to Ipswich. When they came back all parcelled up and so forth, it was my job to get on the trade bicycle - it was one of those bicycles that had a small front wheel, ordinary back wheel and a great big box at the front. I used to load it all in there and go whizzing around Leiston on the bicycle delivering all the dry cleaning to everyone.

And that's where I first came in contact with what we called the 'do-as-you-like' school, up near the station. Its real name was Summerhill, and some people also called it the 'free-and-easy'. I had to deliver both there, and to some people who worked there but lived

## East Suffolk County Education Committee.

Day School No.

Senior School

LEISTON.

Date 27/4/36 193

This is to certify that Harold "Clifford Rouse of
Hayling's Road, Leiston, attended this school for about
four years, leaving to take up an appointment in
the town.

The last year of his school life was spent in the senior class
where he was one of the best scholars we have had for a
long time.

He was good at all his work, especially arithmetic;
was very neat and careful and took a pride in all he
did. He bore an excellent character and his behaviour
was exemplary

Signed

Thos N Clegg
BA (Lond)

*School reference probably obtained prior to Harold's move from Burrage's to the Garrett's office at Leiston Works* in a large house on Haylings Road - and they had two big Alsatians I might add. The Andersons they were.

We'd heard all sorts of tales about Summerhill, how the boys used to run around with knives, how they never did any classes or lessons and so forth, with girls as well as boys up there. And so I felt a bit apprehensive about going there. Walking up the big drive and seeing all these children out doing everything, I remember thinking, 'Oh dear, this is a fine school I'm sure…' But anyway, I did get to know it in time, and there was no problem as far as I was concerned. In fact, I got quite friendly with one lad, he was from India I think, I got to know him quite well.

### Move into an office (May 1936)

Unbeknown to me, Dad had always got it in the back of his mind that I should get into clerical work, because he knew that I was good at arithmetic - that I liked using figures. He came home one night from work and said, 'Would you like to work in an office?' I said, 'Yes, I don't mind, I think I'd like it.' So he said, 'Well, there's a vacancy coming up in the office at the engineering works.'

Dad knew Mr Nunn, the chief storekeeper on the works at Garrett's, Freddie Nunn. He said, 'I had a word with him, and he's drafted out an application for you, if you'd like to copy that out and send it in.' So I did that, and I got the interview with Mr Bamburgh, who was the general manager. Quite a nice chap, I got to know him quite well over time. I had my interview, and I got the job.

My wage at the shop had been five shillings a week, but at the works it came to 6 shillings a week from the start. So I thought, that's a 20 per cent increase. I had to give a week's notice to Mr Burrage of course, and then on the Monday after that, I started in the office. Office boy. That would be 1936, when I was 15 - it was just after my birthday, if I remember rightly – and I started at the beginning of May.

My job involved going in before everybody else in the morning, about half past eight, to get the mail. I opened all the general mail, but anything addressed to individuals I had to put on one side. And then Mr Tonge came in, who was the sort of Company Secretary (I found out later he was also a qualified cost accountant) and he used to take over, then I had to just shoot the mail round the various departments.

At about half past ten in the morning I had to make the tea for everyone in the office. Sometimes I even had to make sandwiches for Mr Bamburgh, particularly when Mr Willmott, the managing director, came down from London - I had to go out and get bread, butter and ham, make sandwiches for them, and take that in to them.

I don't think anyone had coffee in those days, it was all tea. Some had it with sugar, some without, one or two had it without milk... I had a little room where there was a big urn to heat the water, and I used to take the tea round on trays, both downstairs and upstairs in the drawing office.

At about half past eleven, I had to go round again and collect up all the dirty cups, then I had to go outside to the house which was next to the works, where the chief draughtsman, Mr St John Smith (a very nice chap, Scottish) lived with his wife (also nice). There was a scullery where I washed up all the crockery and so forth. The kitchen was next to that, and Mrs St John Smith had a girl who had been to school at the same time as me - I can't remember her name now - she used to work in the kitchen while I was in the scullery. The window and the door faced into a little yard, a little alleyway really, and the window of our telephone exchange was also there, where the telephonist Kathleen was. And for some unknown reason, while I was doing the washing up, I used to sing - just for my own amusement more than anything else.

In the afternoons, I had to get the mail that was going to be posted, lick and stick all the stamps on, write up the stamps I'd used, having perhaps gone in the morning to the post office and bought all the stamps. And so I had a bit of accounting to do myself, even at that stage. I always had to get over to the post office by six o'clock at night and make sure the parcels were in the post that night.

Once a month, all the accounts that were being paid, the purchasing invoices, had to be collected together with the cheques, to be sent up to Mr Willmott in London for him to sign - and they all came back later on for distribution and for posting. So that was my start of office life, and really, I quite enjoyed it.

Well in the Christmas of that year, 1936, unbeknown to me at first, they'd made a collection, in both top and bottom offices, to give to me. But to get it, I had to sing. They all gathered in the bottom office to listen to me sing. I sang *When the Poppies Bloom Again*, I remember that quite well. Evidently it went all right, but I was very nervous, I don't mind admitting. And I got my Christmas box. I don't quite remember now what it amounted to, but I do know it was in cash, and it was very handy.

In about April or May of 1937, I was promoted into the cost office and I was given a job on the stock control section. There was a great big unit with cards in, it was where all the requisitions used to come to be classified, priced and so forth ready to be taken off the records, and we dealt with the purchasing invoices for goods as well. It was quite an interesting job, I enjoyed doing that.

Well, Mr Frederick Chaston, who I worked under, became quite ill - that would be in late 1937 - and he had to be off work, in fact he went into hospital. And Mr Tonge the cost accountant called me in, and he said, 'Now Harold (he called me Harold), now that Mr Chaston has had to go into hospital, do you think you'll be able to manage on the stock ledger by yourself? 'Well I think so, sir.' So he said, 'All right, if there's any problem, come in to me and we'll sort it out.' He was a qualified cost accountant, as Mr Bamburgh was. So I said 'Right.'

By that time, another young lad called John Harris had also joined us on that section - he lived with his widowed mother at Middleton. He was a sort of junior to me. So I was given the job of running that particular section, and I quite enjoyed it.

Freddie Chaston recovered after a time and came back midway through 1938, June or July. So he could take over again, he moved me into the costing area under the chief cost clerk Reg Clark. And that sort of led me onto thinking, right, because Mr Tonge was a member of the Cost & Works Accountants and so was Mr Bamburgh the general manager, if I want to get on in life, I'm going to have to get qualified. But I didn't do anything about it at that stage because the war came and I was only 18 at the time...

## A girl named Dorothy

I met my future wife on the 23rd January 1937 when I was still only 15. It was a Saturday.

At that stage I'd been having dance lessons at Leiston with John Ovens, my friend, in the top room of the White Horse Hotel (in 1933, my sister Connie had had her wedding reception up there - so I knew the place). The Powells at that stage had left - they'd sold up the White Horse Hotel and moved elsewhere in Leiston. Anyway, that's where the dance lessons were held.

After about a fortnight or three weeks, about six of us - John Ovens, myself and Harry Cooper, Mollie and Dulcie Dunn and I can't remember the other girl's name - we decided we'd hire a taxi and go down to the dances we knew were being held on the Saturday night at Aldeburgh, in Jubilee Hall. Mr Lunnis was the taxi driver, and he took us down there, to the dance hall.

The hall had a stage where the refreshments were served at the interval - it led up to the ladies' toilets and downstairs to the gents' toilets. We were down on the floor and the

*Jubilee Hall, Aldeburgh, modern view*

17

*Volunteer PH, Leiston, modern view*

band was on a little dais in the corner - the Walshes - Mr Walsh, Mrs Walsh, he played the trumpet, she played the violin, Fred Clark who was a publican from Leiston at the Volunteer in Haylings Road, he played the piano, and Eddie Kersey, who lived opposite us in Central Road, he played the drums. It was the four of them. The band started up, the foxtrot I think, and John Ovens and myself were sort of looking round for a partner. We saw these two young ladies on the stage, so we said all right, let's go and ask.

And so I asked the girl on the right, who was rather shy, and he asked the other young lady on the left. We got on the floor and danced, and had a little talk as we danced around. It turned out to be Dorothy, and she said the other girl, Phyllis, was her cousin.

I told her we'd come in a group of six, and asked if the two of them would like to join us for the evening, which they did. The two girls spent the rest of the evening in our company, and during the interval, we got them tea or coffee and something to eat. I suppose I danced most of the time with Dorothy - although I think I might have had one dance with Mollie Dunn, who went to school with me (Dulcie was a bit older).

Anyway, that's where it started, and one thing led to another. Those dances were held quite regularly, and after a few times seeing her there, I started to meet her at other times too.

*Dorothy Chase, pictured around 1937*

18

Funnily enough, Mum had asked to come down with me to one of those dances (much to John's amusement - he thought she was coming to spy on me). What transpired was that a Mr Peake used to run those dances down at Aldeburgh. He used to keep a greengrocer's and general grocery store in Haylings Road, and Mother knew Mr Peake quite well, and long before I was old enough to go dancing, he used to ask Mum to go down to do the refreshments there - which she did regularly.

Apparently, before the New Year of 1926, he'd said to Mum, 'Well, we're having a New Year's Eve dance and I want a young lad to be the New Year - do you think you could let your son Harold be it? Mum had thought and said, 'Well yes, of course.' So it was arranged for Dad, Mum and me to all go down to the dance, and we were going to stay overnight in a house Mr Peake owned on the Crag Path at Aldeburgh. So Mum got me dressed in a white shirt, black shorts and I had a big '1926' sash on[*]. Mr Peake said to me, 'When we get down to Aldeburgh, all you've got to do, Harold, is this: when it comes to midnight and we all shout 'Midnight!', I want you to chase the Old Man Time out of the room.' So midnight came, I chased the Old Man Time out, and people cheered and so forth, although I didn't know what was going on really. When the dance was over, all three of us went down to the house Mr Peake had on the Crag Path, and stayed the night then went back home on the Sunday. What I didn't know at that time was that my brother Bertie had done exactly the same thing in 1921, the year that I was born.

Eventually, I was introduced to Dorothy's family (and vice versa), and we spent time in each other's homes in both Leiston and Aldeburgh. She'd got a young brother who was only 18 months old, a sister who was two and a half years younger than Dorothy (who was the eldest). And her father, he was a milkman then. I obviously told her about our family and so forth. We used to go for long walks and

---

[*] This sash is visible in the photograph of Harold aged four on page 7

bike rides*, and in the summer, we took picnics - often stopping on the way at Whitehouse's, the sweet shop next to Leiston picture house, where we used to buy sixpenny bars of Cadbury milk.

In 1938 I got a holiday from the works and Dorothy got a holiday from her job, and we went up to Norwich and spent a week with my sister Connie. She lived at Margetson Avenue in Thorpe St Andrew, and had her baby daughter Ann then. She had first come to the city some years earlier when she was in service at The Deanery, and had now settled there with her husband Billy. Anyway, it was on this visit that we had some photos taken at Jerome's in London Street. I was in my blue striped suit with buttonhole on, Dorothy had a big buttonhole on with her little hat she had and her coat, and I think people thought we were getting married that day!

From Connie and Billy's home at Margetson Avenue in those days we could get a number 80 bus, at Morse Avenue just off Harvey Lane, down into the city. It was silly, but I used to keep all the ticket stubs so I knew how much we spent on the bus. Sometimes we walked one way and took the bus back.

We had the whole week in Norwich, and went to two or three of the cinemas. It's when we really fell in love with Norwich if you like. Dorothy said to me that she'd like to live in Norwich when she was older, and I said, 'Funnily enough, so would I.' We sort of left the idea there for the time being, although we did go back there a number of times until the war broke out.

Ann had been born in 1938, so she was only a few months old on that first visit of ours to Norwich.

My sisters Connie and Louie had become pregnant at roughly the same time. Louie was living at Woodbridge at the time with her husband Reg, and they used to come home to Leiston for the weekend. Going back, I remember once, Connie and Louie were there, I was out in the back yard at Central Road, the window was wide open, and they were talking about their future babies. So I knew about it then, but of

---

* See the map in Appendix 2

course, with Mother it was all hush-hush that they were expecting. Obviously, I did tell Dorothy they were both pregnant. Ann was born in the February, and Barry arrived in the April of 1938.

We were out walking from the autumn and the winter of 1937 onwards, and I remember we used to walk up the Leiston Road in Aldeburgh, up the pathway over the railway line there, and eventually out to the Thorpeness Road. There was a stile halfway along that we used to sit on, and we used to look at the stars. And we picked

*Seventeen-year-old Harold and Dorothy, studio photo taken in Norwich in 1938*

out - I think it's the Little Bear they call it - sort of four in a square and a little one off - and they were our stars - we always called them our stars. Little things I remember. And when we went out, we used to take two tennis rackets with us and a tennis ball, out on the common, and just hit the ball about. We also took a draughts board and a pack of cards and play patience and so forth. And we had our cans of tea to drink – there were no flasks in those days.

**The lead-up to war**

At Aldeburgh, on the last Monday of August, they always used to have a regatta, with a carnival and all the rest of it. Well, 1938 was the last one they had before the war, and even that was a bit dismal because it was the year that Chamberlain had come back waving his piece of paper and saying 'Peace in our time'. They'd still held a regatta, but it wasn't quite the same - even the street lights were dimmed. We had to get busy on air-raid precautions thereafter. By the time we got to 1939, war was imminent and no-one wanted to think about organising a regatta that time, so that was it.

On September 3rd 1939, the day that war broke out, I was at home, I was intending to go down to see Dorothy later on, but I remember listening to the radio at 11 o'clock and hearing Chamberlain announcing that we were now at war with Germany. And of course, we had already been issued during that year with these gas masks - a little tiny fold-up box it was, with string, which we were told to always carry with us no matter where we went. So I put mine on and cycled down to Aldeburgh. We went out on our bikes, I think, somewhere around Aldeburgh - or maybe we went out out for a walk, because we used to do a lot of walking as well.

At that stage, brother Bertie and I were sharing a bedroom – it was normally his room. I'm not quite sure why, because the middle bedroom was empty, but that doesn't matter - I think it must have been because Mum left that for Dorothy when she came over at the weekends, so I kept in with Bertie. We were asleep, when suddenly the works hooter, called the bull, went off - it was the air-raid warning!

It went off about one o'clock in the morning I think it must have been, it woke us all up, and we sort of got up, and then there was a loud banging on our back door. It was the next-door neighbour, frightened out of her life. She had two young boys, her husband was working away, Anne Harvey was her name, and she was so frightened by this, we brought her in with us. We sort of held her hand in the living room until the all-clear went.

I think that was just a practice one actually, that's all it was. We never heard any aircraft anyway. That was our first experience of air-raid sirens. Well, it wasn't actually a siren, it was this bull they called it - a hooter on the boiler house in the top works. It used to sound at ten to eight in the morning and eight o'clock in the morning for the start of work, and again at lunchtime, and again at knocking-off time at half past five. They made that the air-raid warning for the time being, but later on, they did have proper sirens fitted. That was our first experience of what war was going to bring upon us, really.

**Joining up** (December 1939)

As quite a young boy, perhaps seven or eight, I was very interested in aeroplanes as a means of transport. In fact, most of my reading on the First World War dealt with the air side of that - not because of the fighting in the air, but because of the aeroplanes themselves - I was always very interested in that aspect.

Well, one day we learned that a squadron of the RAF had come down and landed in a field near to the road on the way to Aldeburgh, with some biplane fighter planes - I think they were Hawker Harts. Dad was away from work at the time because he had poisoned his hand with a rusty nail, cutting some wood. He and I walked down to this place half-way to Aldeburgh. I think there were six aircraft there, so half a squadron by the looks of it, as I learned later on. This must have been 1928 or 1929.

There was one of the aeroplanes where people were allowed to get close and have a good look. I can remember Dad lifting me up so I could see inside the cockpit. I was fascinated by this. In fact, I remember someone came pushing in and tried to sort of pull me off, and Dad spoke to them and told them to leave me for a minute or two. I was absolutely thrilled to see that plane, and if anything, it encouraged me more.

23

I got onto reading *Biggles* stories, which I did, avidly. Then Mum allowed me to have the *Aviation* magazine every week, which was so interesting. It was after that that I saved up my pocket money and bought a Meccano aeroplane construction set - so I was able to make a couple of biplanes and a seaplane. I also bought a little pilot to go in the cockpit.

I always thought, 'I shall never be able to afford to fly, but perhaps when I'm old enough I will join the RAF.' Of course, that's one thing that Mother would never allow - she definitely put her foot down about that. But when war did come along and I did join up, she didn't object at all. But I do know she didn't *like* it.

I've mentioned this to show that I'd always wanted to fly, and in 1939, it so happened I was at a point when it looked like I had the opportunity to do so - under circumstances which I wish hadn't happened, but there you are - there was a war on, and that was it.

So my brother Bertie and I decided to join up. We had to go to the recruiting office in Ipswich for our medicals, and Bertie went up first. I think it was the first week of December 1939. I went up a week later, and they said right, we'll let you know when we want you for call-up.

However, in the meantime, my sister Louie had gone down with tuberculosis, and she was in this special hospital, a sanatorium on the outskirts of Ipswich*. When I went there to join up, Dorothy came with me - she waited out in the town somewhere while I went through the medical and so forth.

Then we went together out to the sanatorium to see Louie. We'd bought a teddy bear for her son Barry, because he was coming up to his second birthday. We went and saw her, and she was in bed in this big room wide open to the atmosphere - that's how they used to treat them. And oh dear, she looked terrible, she really did. We stayed with her three quarters of an hour, or something like that. She couldn't talk much, and we reported back to Mum and Dad when we got back to Leiston.

---

* The sanatorium was at Foxhall, east of the town

On January 15th 1940, Dorothy had spent the weekend in Leiston with me, and Mum and Dad had gone off to see Louie at the sanatorium on the Sunday. They didn't say much when they got back. Dorothy was staying at ours on the Sunday night, but she was going on the early morning bus back to Aldeburgh to work. As we were getting ready to go that morning, Mum said to me, 'While you're down at the post office square waiting for the bus, do you mind phoning up the sanatorium and finding out how Louie is?' I said all right, I will.

*Connie (right) with her vivacious sister Louie, pictured around 1931*

So we got down there in time so I could go in the telephone kiosk. I phoned up the sanatorium and was told that she'd died that night, in the early hours of that morning.

Then Bertie and I got our calling up papers, and we were told we were going off on the Wednesday 17th. And on Tuesday 16th, Reg (Louie's husband) asked whether she could be brought back to Central Road - which she was, in the front room. Mum took me in there on the Tuesday to see her, but it wasn't very pleasant.

Overnight on that Tuesday and Wednesday, we had a terrific snowstorm, and Bertie and I needed to catch the 8.00 train from Leiston. We were to look out at Ipswich for the Flight Sergeant from the recruiting office, who'd have some more papers for us.

Bertie was still working for Herbert Ives then (the gentleman's outfitters in Leiston) and so we bought ourselves a pair of wellington boots each because of the snow - we needed to wear those going up to the station. Dad came with us carrying our shoes. We took the wellingtons off when we got to the station and put our shoes on, and off we went.

We saw the Flight Sergeant at Ipswich Station who had been wandering around looking for us. He said, 'Right, you're going to Uxbridge.' Well, I'd been up to London on a cheap day return three or four times with Dorothy (five shillings return on a Sunday), but I didn't really know the place. However, I thought I knew about the Tube and I'd find my way there. I don't think Bertie even knew that.

## Uxbridge (January 1940)

We got there, to Uxbridge*, and luckily the station wasn't very far away from the RAF station gate. It wasn't an aerodrome, just a camp. We walked in, booked in, and we were shown to a great big barracks with a lot of other lads all up there.

We were going to sleep that night in a large dormitory-type building, and they said there would be an evening meal served at…I think it was six o'clock, something like that. They told us how to get down to the food hall. There were a lot of other lads who had also come up on the train that day from other places, so it was quite a number of us. We all went down to the food hall, where there was a long table. The ones sitting closest to the serving hatch had to get the food in a great big container and dish it out to the rest of us in turn. That was all new to us, obviously. We had a decent hot meal anyway, then a sweet, and a mug of tea.

Then it was back to the sleeping 'hut' - quite a big building actually - I think we were up on the first floor. We were told where the NAAFI† was, so we could go there in the evening. Even though we weren't in uniform, we were allowed in. So I think we spent some time in the NAAFI that night before going off to bed.

---

* See map in Appendix 6 for all the RAF locations mentioned in this book
† Navy, Army and Air Force Institutes provided catering and leisure services

The ablutions were on the same floor as us, in part of the corridors - there were baths, but mainly wash basins. We got into our pyjamas, and were told to pack all of our civilian clothes into our cases, because the cases would be taken off us the following day and sent on the train back home - we were to be issued with our uniforms.

We woke up at reveilles but were still in our civilian clothes the following day. We went to another building, where we had to line up. That's where we took the oath and we were 'chested', i.e. given our number - these were issued roughly alphabetically. Bertie's number was 911639 and I got 911641. Someone else had got in the middle of us (911640), so there was a bit of a gap between the two of us - but that was neither here nor there.

After we were sworn in, they told us we were all going to be trained as wireless operators, which they were urgently requiring - they knew they were going to be having some big bombers, but we didn't know that. 'However,' they said, 'at the moment we've got nowhere to put you on the training course. Now, you have the choice - you can stay with us and do whatever jobs we give you and go wherever we say, or you can go back on deferred service.'

With Louie's funeral service coming up on Saturday, Bertie and I decided we'd go back on deferred service, thinking it might be a few days or weeks before they called us back. Two other lads also said they'd go on deferred service. So they gave us a little lapel badge to have to show that we were in the RAF but on deferred service, and we took our own suitcases back home with us.

Once again, it was back on the Tube to Liverpool Street. I remember we had to change somewhere, and getting onto the other platform, the train had already arrived and was just about to leave, but I dashed in as the doors were going to close. Bertie was well behind me but the doors couldn't close, and so we both got in.

We got to Liverpool Street, and made it back home in the snow and slush, and walked in on Mum and Dad. They didn't expect to see us. In fact, I went on down to Aldeburgh that night to see Dorothy as well. (I think we must have arrived on the earlier train, because I remember going back up to Leiston Station again to get the train to Aldeburgh to see Dorothy - but I came back later on the bus, because the trains had stopped running by then.) Anyway, I managed to get down and give her a surprise.

After all that, in the end, we didn't get recalled until June.

**Biding time** (January to June 1940)

From that January until the June, I sort of had the normal life I'd had before. They were still holding the dances down at Aldeburgh and at Snape, I think - I don't know about the Thorpeness one - and Dorothy and I still managed to go out for a picnic on Sundays on our bicycles, or for walks. And she came over to Leiston for the weekend. We used to walk up the Saxmundham Road, round to Knodishall and all over - it must be 7 or 8 miles I should think.

I'd originally told them at the works that I was going in the RAF, they had wished me goodbye and all the rest of it, but on the Monday, I walked back in again.

Bertie went back to Herbert Ives - well, only for a few days, that's the thing - he'd given in his notice and decided to go freelance. He went from there to Freeman Hardy & Willis, and ended up going round the country for them doing relief work at various shops. He used to come home at weekends though, and I remember one Sunday he and I rode down to Sizewell to view a boat that had been torpedoed off the coast - it was quite a way out, but you could just about see it at the horizon.

# PART II: Life in the services

## RAF Compton Bassett (June 1940)

In due course, we got our calling up papers to report to somewhere called Compton Bassett. I'd never heard of the place. However, John Ovens' father, who was a gatekeeper on the top works, I knew that he came from that part of the world, Wiltshire. So I made my way up there, and I said, 'Oh, Mr Ovens, I think you know Wiltshire...', and he said 'Yes,' so I said, 'Compton Bassett?' 'Oh yes' he said, 'it's near Calne, and Swindon'. I said, 'That's where we've been called up', and he said 'Oh, they must be building a place there, because there wasn't an aerodrome, so far as I know.'

By June, Dunkirk had already happened, and there was a lot being said about that. I'd said my goodbye to Dorothy on Sunday 16<sup>th</sup> down at Aldeburgh, and we'd had our little talk about this, that and the other. On the Monday, Bertie and I were on the train again. Funnily enough, John Ovens, who'd come back from Dunkirk, was on leave, and he came up to the station to see us off. (He and Phyllis, Dorothy's cousin, went on to get married later that summer.)

When we got the train at Paddington, a lot of other lads got on as well, so there was quite a group of us. We had to change at Chippenham to get the train to Calne. When we got off there, we couldn't help noticing a Harris sausage factory right outside the station - you could certainly smell it. There was a young corporal who met us and when we said, 'Cor blimey, what a smell!', he said, 'Don't worry, you'll be having them for breakfast, lunch and tea!' He then ordered us to get into lines of three, and marched us on narrow winding back lanes past all the fields to the camp at Compton Bassett. It was a brand-new camp, and we were the first ones there.

Once again, it wasn't actually an aerodrome, just a camp, and ours was Hut C3. It was quite nice and took about 24 of us I suppose - twelve of us each side.

There were three groups of brothers in our hut. There was Bertie and me, the Dowsetts... and I can't remember the third pair. The Dowsett brothers were real cockneys, one was very short and the other very tall. We all got nicknames quite quickly. Bertie's initials were B.A.G., so he got called 'Bag'. Because mine were H.C., I was 'Hot and Cold', and so on.

There was a little room at the end for the corporal or whoever was in charge of the hut. Bert and I were side by side, but alternate beds were the other way around - one was head to the wall, the next one was head to the middle, and so on. Well, Bertie got the one with its head to the middle: he didn't like that, so he made up his bed the other way round. Every time we had a bed inspection or hut inspection, which was quite often, he had to quickly change it round - not the whole bed, but the bed clothes.

*Bertie and his little brother Harold, studio portrait, 1940*

Our daily routine involved our basic training, square-bashing as we called it - PT* and all the rest of it.

Then sometime in the July, Bertie complained of something, some pain. He went to the Medical Officer, and they promptly took him to Yatesbury, about 4 miles up the road, where they had a hospital. It wasn't pleurisy, but something similar, and he was in there about a fortnight.

In the meantime, I'd been receiving rifle drill ready for doing guard duty and so forth, and the day that Bertie came back from Yatesbury was the day I'd been detailed to be on guard duty at the main gate. I told Bertie that I was going to report to the gate at 6 o'clock that night. Bertie said, 'I can do that for you, you don't have to do it. My name is Rouse, they won't know anything about it!' I said, 'Look, you haven't done all the training.' He said, 'That's all right, I've got the rifle, I'll go down there.' So he took over the duty. Evidently, he did get in a bit of a muddle at one point, because an officer came past him and he didn't quite know what to do! But he got away with it, and I got away with it too - because, of course, I could have been in trouble as well.

Later on, we had our first evening out in Calne. As we were walking there, at one point the path went up high whereas the road stayed low. We saw an officer coming down on his bicycle, and he said something to us - I thought he'd said 'OK'. But Bertie, who'd had his pipe in his mouth, told me what he actually said was 'Your pipe!' Luckily, nothing else happened about that. We carried on into Calne and found the local pub.

Then there was the occasion when it was a Sunday, and Bertie, Ginger Munson and myself decided to go out into the village. We knew that the Women's Institute (I think it was) had a hut there which they'd turned into a canteen for services, so we said we'd go over there and have an afternoon cup of tea. Of course, when we got there, we discovered it didn't open until 4 o'clock. Just then, these two young

---

* Physical Training (also called PE, Physical Exercise)

girls came walking along, and Bertie, being Bertie, jokingly said 'Oh, that's very nice of your parents to invite us back for tea'. Well, they sniggered and walked off, and we sort of wandered along behind them.

After some way, these two girls turned into a gateway of a nice little cottage, so I said all right, and we turned round to come away. But just then, one of the girls came back out again and said, 'Yes, Mum and Dad have invited you in for tea!' So the two of us went in for tea. And over the weeks that followed Bertie got rather friendly with that girl - that is, until he grew his little moustache... Then she said to him, 'Well, if you're going to keep that little moustache, I'm not going to see you again', so Bertie said 'Well I *am* going to keep the moustache...!' On one of my photographs[*] he's got that moustache on. Dear oh dear... that was my brother for you.

We'd been there six weeks altogether when we got our first weekend leave, lasting from after duty on Saturday until midnight on Sunday - so not very long. Our hut got together and we ordered a coach to come to the gates to take us up to London - it was the quickest way, you see. We all got on the coach and off to London we went. We got the last train home from Liverpool Street at 5.21 or whatever it was, and we'd be home by 8 o'clock.

I'd written to Dorothy to say I'd be home that weekend, and so she came to Saxmundham to meet us. We went home, and I think Dorothy must have stayed the night at Leiston and gone back on Sunday - we had to catch the train at 3.40 on Sunday afternoon to get back in time to pick up the coach on the Embankment. We were back in camp by midnight on Sunday, so that was OK.

Six weeks after that, we got another weekend pass. But this time on the Saturday morning, before we collected our passes, they threw a gas drill at us. We had to put on our capes, our masks and all that stuff, and once that was over, we had to strip back. Bertie said, 'Now, I really must have a good wash,' but everyone else told him to come on and hurry. This time the coach had been barred from coming to the

---

[*] See page 30

front gate, so it had to come to a side gate. We were late leaving, but we made it as far as the west side of London at Ealing Broadway (where the Central Line comes to), and there the coach driver dropped us. Most of us were wanting Liverpool Street because we came from that sort of area.

We got on the Tube to Liverpool Street, and arrived on the platform in time to see the train disappearing up the line. We were just too late, mainly because of Bertie's delay back at camp - although the

*Harold shows off his new uniform in the rear garden of 53 Central Road, Leiston, while Bertie and his proud mother look on*

driver had done very well trying to get us there in time.

At the top of the road opposite Liverpool Street platform 9, there was a Forces canteen, so we went there to get a tea and bun, something like that, and while we were in there, the sirens went off. This was September 7th 1940. We all dashed out and saw the German planes overhead, saw the fighters coming in to fight them and all the rest of it - we didn't really think about bombs dropping or anything like that - but they plastered Barkingside and the docks that night.

The next train that we could catch didn't leave until just gone 7 o'clock, and although we managed to get on it, it absolutely crawled along. It took ages to get past Shenfield, and we saw all the flames and smoke from the bombing, so we knew London had got plastered that night.

At last, we got down to Ipswich - it must have been about 11 o'clock I should think, and of course we couldn't get any further. We spoke to the station porter and he said the first train we would be able to catch would be the mail train at 6.30 in the morning or something like that. We asked him what we could do now. He said the best thing he could advise was to walk out of the station and try the police station further down the road. Bertie and I went down, explained the situation, and the policeman said, 'I can put you up,' and he promptly put us in a cell!

So we stayed in a cell that night, and he said they'd wake us up in time to go for the train, which they did. They even gave us a cup of tea before we went up to the railway station. We caught the train - and of course it stopped at every station on the way down. We could get as far as Saxmundham, but not to Leiston - so we had to get the bus for the last bit of the trip.

That night, the Home Guard had been put on standby duty, because they thought the invasion had started. We finally arrived outside the White Horse Hotel on the corner in Leiston, and there was a whole group of Dad's Army people there. When we got off the bus, there was a chap I'd gone to school with asking me for identification. I said, 'You idiot, you know me, I went to school with you!' He said, 'Never mind that, my officer is standing right behind me!'

I finally got home, and I said to Mum, 'Right, I'm off to Aldeburgh.' I got my bicycle out again, pedalled off, but then had to come back again a short time later, because we had to catch the 4 o'clock train back again on Sunday.

We got to Liverpool Street, then had to go over to Embankment - where our coach was picking us up right outside what used to be New Scotland Yard (before they'd moved to where they are now). The driver was going to leave at 8 o'clock on the dot. In fact, he'd told us, 'I'm not waiting one second after 8 o'clock - so if anyone's not here, too bad.'

Anyway, we got in the coach, and by that time the sirens had gone off again and bombs were falling. The only one who didn't make it was Ron Angel, who lived at Ipswich. We had seen him on the train, but last glimpsed him walking up the Embankment on his own towards the coach - but the driver wouldn't wait for him.

We were getting out of London as bombs were falling, such as when we passed through Knightsbridge while they were bombing the barracks there. The coach driver said, 'Right, duck down and put your overcoat over your head, in case the windows come in,' which we did. He weaved his way through and we got out to Eton Broadway again, which was quieter, and finally arrived back at camp just before midnight.

It was our first direct experience of bomb raids, really. The driver did marvellously well to get us that far. Well, Ron did eventually get back to camp early the next morning. He explained what had happened, and fortunately for him, they didn't put him on extra duties or anything like that.

I remember another occasion when we were at Calne, Bertie and I went down to Bath - where all the Admiralty officers were sent. We went down there a couple of times on the Sunday. On the first time we went down, we found this forces canteen which the girls (Admiralty typists and so forth) were billeted in, and they had turned the basement into a services café. There was a room with a table tennis table, and I think there was a card table as well. Anyway, at 10 o'clock, that closed down and you had to leave.

But once again, brother Bertie was up to his tricks. A couple of girls said look, there is an attic up there, and when we say time to go at 10 o'clock, wait here, we'll let everyone out, and you four can stay. That's how we became members of what they called the basement club. We were allowed to go up to the attic and sleep there, and then the girls called us the next morning so we could catch the train back to Chippenham. And then from Chippenham to Calne, I remember we had to walk along the railway line because there wasn't a train. Anyway, we got back to camp before 8 o'clock roll call all right.

Another night, we were down there when there was a bombing raid on Bath. We went out into the streets to see if there was anything we could do, although we had no tin hats or anything. We were crazy, I suppose. But there was not much we could do - the bombing was a bit further away from where we were, so we went back.

Then in September, when we'd got up to 12 words a minute on the Morse, I passed the test, but Bertie didn't, and actually I think he failed on purpose. Unlike me, Bertie didn't want to go aircrew, and in any case, he'd already decided he didn't want to become a wireless operator. I was being sent for my air training, so we were going our separate ways.

Bertie left Compton Bassett a little while after that. I forget exactly where he went then - it was down to RAF Benson, I think. In due course, he ended up at Cranwell on the equipment course. Being in the trade of men's outfitters and so on, I suppose that suited him better. He got through that course all right and was made up to a corporal, eventually. He then got posted to various places, and ended up in Yorkshire, and that's where he first met his future wife Dorothy.

### RAF Yatesbury (September 1940)

I went for the medical for aircrew, got through, and was posted up to Yatesbury for the first of my air training[*]. This was to carry on with the Morse to get up to 18 words a minute and do a bit more technical work as well.

It was the first time that I had flown. We went up in biplanes, the Dominie, a De Haviland - they used it for charter flights in those days in civilian life. I think it had three seats for trainee wireless operators, along with their sets and an instructor. We had to do various exercises

---

[*] No.2 Signal School Yatesbury

De Haviland Dominie,
1940s

while we were flying, and then came back. Of course, we were each fitted up with a special parachute - not just a harness, it was a sort of tunic thing with a parachute.

It was after I had started there, and I can't remember how it happened, but I suddenly developed acute toothache - affecting one of my lower teeth. I had to report to one of the dental people, and he said, 'Oh, we'll have to have that out.' So he said to his nurse, 'Right, get him on the table...' Evidently, that tooth had a bulbous root, and it took him 20 minutes or more, with the nurse holding my head, while he tried to get it out - but throughout, I never felt a thing, I didn't honestly. However, afterwards, my cheek blew up enormously. The following day I walked back down to Calne, to Compton Bassett, to see Bertie. He was shocked and said, 'What's happened to you?' After I'd told him, I walked back to camp again.

It was my pals Rudd and Smithy and me, and about three others I think, who were going forward as aircrew. The rest were staying on to be trained as wireless operators, mechanics and so forth.

While I was up at Yatesbury, many of the RAF personnel on the station actually lived out at Swindon, and they used to come in on the bus in the morning. I knew that one of the Leiston lads was up there - I knew him by sight, and that his parents lived at Carr Avenue in Leiston. One morning I saw him, a sergeant, and I said, 'Excuse me, you're Sergeant Rowlands, aren't you...?'. He replied, 'Oh yes, I know your brother Bertie quite well.' And he said, 'Would you like to go home on a weekend pass?' I said, 'Well yes I would, but I shan't get one.' He said, 'Yes, you will, I'll see to it for you, but the only thing is, you're to go to see my mum and dad, let them know that I'm all right.' So I said, 'All right, fair enough.'

He got me a weekend pass. I hitched up to London, because we were on the main A4 road, and from there I got the train home. Dorothy came to Leiston for that weekend, and we went up to Carr Avenue. We saw Mr and Mrs Rowlands, and I made myself known.

We met their other son and they were very pleased to see us. We had afternoon tea with them, well, a cup of tea and a piece of cake. I think I must have had to go back on the late train from Leiston that night, because weekend passes were only for Saturday and up to midnight on Sunday in those days, or 23.59 as we used to say.

In the end, I failed my 18 words a minute test, so I had to stay on at Yatesbury, whereas Rudd and Smithy, they both passed. I had passed on the technical side, but it was my speed of Morse that let me down. My pals went off and they were posted up to Lossiemouth, I think, onto OTU (Operational Training Unit), on a January course. So I didn't see them any more after that.

However, I did write to Rudd occasionally, such as when I wanted to let him know when I did finally pass my 18 words a minute, that was just before Christmas of 1940.

I then got posted down to RAF Manston as an AC2 wireless operator (that indicated I'd got my wireless badge) and a trainee gunner. The gunnery schools were apparently all full up at that time, so they weren't ready for me - but they said they'd let me know when there was a vacancy.

### RAF Manston (December 1940)

RAF Manston was a station that had been heavily bombed in the Battle of Britain. It was in two parts - the airfield was on one side, and the signals section on the other. There was a main road that went through between them, that went down to Canterbury eventually. The signals section and the photographic section and things like that were on the opposite side to the airfield.

I think I was the only one that had to go there that day from London - I don't think I met up with anyone. I found my way to Manston - I got off the train at Margate actually, then got the bus. I booked in, and got the billet, the hut I was going to be in - it was just off the parade ground they had there. That had been bombed earlier on - there were craters and potholes here, there and everywhere. I was put in this hut with quite a few others. A lot of the buildings were built over tunnels, and we were told that these were our air raid shelters if anything happened. Well, we did get occasional raids from single aircraft, and when they came over, we did have to go down there.

*Luftwaffe aerial photograph of Manston airfield dated 1939*

I got leave from Manston in January 1941, and went home. By that time, I had all my flying gear with me, so I had two kit bags to see to - all the flying kit in one, and my other stuff in the other. It was quite a lug going through London after the blitz with two kit bags, and I had to tie them round my neck as it was the only way of carrying them, because there were no handles on them.

I was home for the week, and I remember going up into mum's bedroom and dressing myself in all my flying gear to show them. We were given an inner layer of woollen underclothes but I didn't put those on - beautiful underclothes, silken wool, long sleeves, long johns and all the rest of it, and I never did wear them - Dad had them in the end. But I dressed up with outer clothes, flying boots and helmet on, and clomped down the stairs. It was an Irvin suit that we had in those days, very long and all in one, right down to the ankles, padded and what have you, so it looked a bit bulky. I don't think Mum was too happy about seeing me like that, but anyway.

We were told that we were in the signals section but may be called upon to do other duties as well. One day I was given duty in the cookhouse. I don't think I was put on potato-peeling or any cooking – mostly, I did cleaning duties. That particular day was pay day (we got paid fortnightly), and we had to go down the tunnels to get paid. We went down, got into line, and the chap in front of me got called, then me, then the chap behind me, and so forth. So we got our pay and I thought I'll take this back to the billet as I don't want to try and keep it with this overall on. I went back to the billet and put the money in my wallet which was in my tunic hanging up behind the bed - I think it was three one-pound notes and a ten-shilling note. I then returned to finish off my duty in the cookhouse.

That night after evening meal, four or five of us said OK, let's go to the NAAFI and play Bingo (it wasn't called that, there was another name for it - the name given to it made it legal to play in the services). In the NAAFI, they also had drinks, and we agreed we'd all get our own drinks – that was fair enough. I got my wallet out, and there was only a ten-shilling note in there - no pound notes at all. Someone's pinched them.

Well, the chap that had been in front of me and the chap behind me in the pay queue, I said to them, 'We've all got brand new notes, haven't we? You've got the numbers of your notes, so we can work out the three numbers that were mine.' So I went to the guard room, reported this and told them about the numbers on the cash, as it may have been possible to trace the thief.

There had been one chap back in the billet that none of us really took to, a small chap with a mousy face. He'd been off-duty that day and he'd evidently gone into Ramsgate. He came back later that night, and we didn't say anything to him about the theft. One of the lads asked if he'd been out, and he said yes, he'd been shopping and bought a rather nice cigarette case. We thought, that's funny.

So we went and reported this chap and said that we wondered if it was him, but the guard room didn't do anything about it. All they did was report it to the padre, and a couple of days later the padre called me into his office and gave me 30 shillings, I think, from church funds. In the meantime, I'd written home to Dad and told him the sad story and he had sent me a pound or two pounds, so in the end I had my money. But it did leave a sour taste in my mouth. We were all quite certain it was that little chap who did it while there was no-one else around at the billet, and I just wish that the guards at the guardroom had followed it up. We even knew the shop name, and they could have got down there and seen whether the numbers of the notes matched. That always stuck in my gullet. But no, I expect they said it's one of those things - I was a fool and I learned my lesson. I never did that again.

*Harold (front centre) and his pals outside their billet. This photograph was not labelled, but is thought to have been taken at RAF Manston in the Spring of 1941.*

I spent six months at Manston. For the first four months, I was stationed in what used to be a DF[*] station in the middle of a field, some distance away from the camp. Originally, it was there to give direction-finding instructions to the fighter pilots, but at that stage it had been decommissioned and turned into a communications service. There were five of us there - a corporal and four others, AC2s or AC1s like me[†].

We had a shift pattern we worked to, on a sort of a four-day basis. We had a morning shift, an afternoon shift, then a night shift. And after the night shift, we had three days off. When we first went there, I found it quite interesting, sitting on this big radio set listening as we got the messages through, all in code. You had to write it all down - four letter codes, and at the start they tell you how many groups of four there will be - it could be anything from a hundred to five hundred. We had to take them down by Morse, and when done, to phone up the despatch officer down at camp to send a rider on his motorbike. He picked the coded message up and took it back to the intelligence officer.

Once I suddenly got called up, and there was a 500-group message coming through - I know I filled up two sheets of my pad anyway. And right in the middle of it the siren went off. There was firing over at the aerodrome so I knew something was going off. It didn't scare me, but it distracted my attention, so some of the four letter blocks I didn't really get. Anyway, I carried on, got the rest of the message, and we had another station we could call up to say if we'd missed part of the message - they gave it to me, so that was all right. I called up the despatch rider, he came and took the message off to the cipher officer. What it was I don't know, but it was quite a long one. Most others I took were shorter than that.

They used to send a supply of food up to us, and when it was pay day, they used to come up with the pay packets. We never went in the

---

[*] direction-finding
[†] These were aircraftmen grades

main camp - we were left to ourselves. This field was down towards the village, and the only way we could have water was to go down to one of the cottages and get water in two buckets with one of those yokes over our shoulders. We used to take turns to get the water in like that. That included having a wash, having our daily ablutions as best we could, shaving and what have you. We did have an Elsan toilet* there though.

The first time I'd completed my night shift, I thought, 'I've got three days off,' and I said to the corporal, 'I think I'd like to go home.' He said, 'All right,' although I didn't have a pass - but down at the camp they wouldn't know anything about it.

So I used to go home every other four days, and I had quite a few unofficial weekends there. I used to hitch-hike to Margate to get the train to London, then get back to Leiston. People used to say 'Oh, you're home... now when are you going back?' - always, they *always* said that! Although Dorothy and I said we'd write to each other every day, there were occasions when we couldn't, and even when I was certain I could get off, I never used to write that date - so when I walked in, she didn't really know I was coming. The most I used to say was, 'hopefully' I shall be there on whatever date. I spent some time at Leiston and some at Aldeburgh, and that went on for four months or so.

I then got drafted back into the main camp - in the signals section. And I was working with a chap called George Atkin. I knew George because he had been at Yatesbury with me. In fact, he was the first man I ever knew who had an electric razor. It was when I saw it and he said, 'Do you want to try it?', that I first got talking with him. He'd been all round the country doing the electrics on the new cinemas that were opening up, and he'd been working on the cinema at Saxmundham, so he knew the area.

Later on, after the war, he went back to the BBC, and I saw his name up quite a number of times as lighting director. Anyway, I was

---

* This was a type of chemical toilet

43

crewed-up with him, and we used to do repair work. Aircraft that came down in an emergency at Manston often had to be checked over - I did this with George, and enjoyed it.

Well, there was one time when a Whitley had come down - a big black bomber - and George and I had to go over. It was on the outskirts of the airfield. We got there and started working on the electrics and

radio stuff, and while doing that I noticed a squadron of Blenheims crossing over on their way to bomb the other side. An hour later, they started coming back, and one was in trouble - having difficulty with his engine - and he came down and crash-landed off the

*Bristol Blenheim, 1940s*

airstrip, not a hundred yards from where we were working. I said to George, 'Blimey, I'd better see if there's anything I can do', and I ran over to the aircraft.

The three-man crew, the pilot, the navigator and the wireless operator air gunner had all got out of the aircraft, which was on its belly. The pilot had got a shell through the side of his ankle, but the others were not hurt. I was facing two officers and a sergeant, and the officer navigator said to me, 'Oh, there's a camera in there, go inside, get it out and take it to your camera section, get him to produce the photographs.' 'Righto sir', I said, so I went in, unlocked the camera, and did the long walk back to the camp and into the photographic section.

I wasn't quite sure where the photographic section was at the time - it was down a side road beside the guardroom actually. When I got there, I told them I'd been sent with this camera from the Blenheim that's just come down and they want the things developed, so it was 'Right, fair enough.'

Well, the night before, we'd had the ENSA* party at the camp, and they were giving a show. Now I've got to jump back a bit, to the Christmas of 1940, in fact it was just after Christmas, probably the

---

* Entertainments National Service Association

early part of January 1941. I'd had a week's leave, and Dorothy and I went to see a show at the Hippodrome in Norwich - I forget how we got there, but I think we hired a taxi - there was a little group of us all going to the Hippodrome. It was quite a good show. There were four dancing girls, and one of the dancing girls rather struck me, I don't know why - I enjoyed her dancing and I said so to Dorothy at the time - and this dancer sort of stuck in my memory, I suppose. Anyway, when this ENSA party had come down to Manston, it would be at the end of May, on this particular night there were two dancers in the show - and one of them was this same girl.

*Harold in civvies, on a visit to Connie's home in Norwich, March 1941*

While she was in the wings waiting to go on, I asked her, 'Excuse me, but were you dancing in the Hippodrome in Norwich earlier in the year?' and she said 'Yes I was.' I said, 'I thought I recognised you.' We got talking, and later on she said to me, 'We're having a show at Ramsgate tomorrow night, and then they're going to run a dance there, would you like to come down?' I said, 'Well, yes, thank you very much indeed.' They were billeted at Canterbury and were going down to Ramsgate by coach. I would have to go down on my own from the camp. So I thought all right, fair enough. This was the night after I'd taken this camera into the photographic section.

I got to Ramsgate and found the hall where the dance was being held, saw the tail end of the show and then met up with this young lady, and actually had a couple of dances with her. One of the dances had just finished, when suddenly there was an announcement made over the loudspeaker: 'WILL H.C. ROUSE 911641 REPORT IMMEDIATELY BACK TO CAMP.' Oh dear, what have I done? I couldn't think of anything. I said to her, 'I'm sorry, I shall have to go now, that was me they were calling.' She said, 'Crikey, are you in trouble?' I told her I didn't know what it was about...

So back to camp I went, it was three or four miles away, and I reported straight to the guardroom. 'It's H.C. Rouse. I understand you want to see me.' 'Oh yes,' he said, 'We understand you took a camera out of an aircraft, now what did you do with it?' I'd been seen carrying the camera, apparently someone had reported it and thought I was swiping it or something. I said, 'I took it to the photographic section where I was told to take it.' 'Oh?' I said, 'Yes, you check with the photographic section, you'll find that I booked it in there at four o'clock in the afternoon (I think it was) – it was on the instruction of the navigator officer of the Blenheim. I did as I was told.' 'Oh? Wait a minute.' So he checked, and of course found out that I was telling the truth. 'Oh', he said, 'I'm sorry to drag you back.' 'That's all right,' I said, 'I'm back here now, I'll go to bed.'

So that was that. And of course, I never saw that ENSA girl any more, because obviously she was off travelling around the country.


**Back to RAF Yatesbury** (June 1941)

It was just after that that I was called back to Yatesbury, at the end of June 1941 I think it was, to go on a refresher course. At that time, the radio sets in the aircraft had all been changed over, and I needed to go on a refresher course to learn how to use the new equipment.

When I was first trained, the radio sets being used in the aircraft were becoming obsolete, 1082 and 1083 they were called. They were peculiar sets - you had a box with six coils in it, green, red and yellow. You had to put these into the transmitter and also into the receiver, and they governed the band of frequency that you would get. I would be a bind as you put these in – a very complicated thing it was.

In the meantime, the Marconi people had developed a combined transmitter/receiver. It was called the Marconi T1154/R1155, much better, lovely*. They were marvellous sets, with none of those coils or anything like that.

So I completed that training, which took me to the early part of August.


### RAF Jurby (August 1941)

After the refresher course, I was at last posted for my gunnery course - to Jurby on the Isle of Man†, along with a lot of others. Five of us sort of ganged up together, and we called ourselves the 'Squidgeon Club' - don't ask me why.

We got on the train at Calne, changed at Chippenham, and the five of us were travelling in one compartment. It was going to be a night journey up to Fleetwood, it must have been, and we needed our sleep. So two of us got in the top luggage rack, two of us were sleeping on the seats and I slept on the floor in the middle. We went into Bristol, kept on the same train, and carried on up to Fleetwood.

We had our photograph taken along the seafront in Fleetwood, members of the Squidgeon Club, and we each kept a copy. It was one of those quick photograph things taken by a street photographer, and I kept that particular photograph for a long time, until after the war, although I'm not sure what happened to it. Of course, I never met any of the others again, because we all got split up after a while. But in that photograph, funnily enough, my face was the only one you could really see - the others somehow got blacked out, and they are the ones who all got killed... but my face was still there.

In the morning we walked onto the ship. It was a bit rough that day, but fortunately the sea-sickness didn't affect me, and we got to Douglas in the Isle of Man. They said we'd have to catch the train to get over to Jurby, but there won't be one for a couple of hours or something like that, so we had time to have a look round Douglas.

---

* This equipment is visible on the photograph of the Lancaster interior on page 72
† This was No.5 Air Observer School (AOS) Jurby

So we walked along the front at Douglas, and we came across a wire fence, a tall one, with lots of people behind it, and they all started shouting and spitting at us. They were apparently civilians of various nationalities, including Germans, who had been rounded up and put in there for security reasons. And they didn't like it - I didn't know how long they were there…

Anyway, we got on the train, a funny little train, which took us up to Jurby, where the airfield was. We got off there, and we were put in tents on the outskirts of the aerodrome, the five of us all in a bell tent. Being under canvas was all right though, because it was fine weather the whole time we were there.

We quickly started our gunnery course there - it was quite intensive, because the course normally took a year, and we had to do it in about three weeks. It included flying in Blenheims with guns firing at a drogue, and then doing exercises on the ground dismantling the guns and so forth. So that went through, we all qualified, and we all became sergeants, wireless operator air gunners.

It was quite a nice day when we had our half-wings presented, together with our stripes. Most of us sewed our stripes onto our tunic and great coat with our half wing that we had, but one chap didn't - he said he didn't think he'd bother about that. By that time, we'd moved into the town on the north side of the Isle of Man (I can't think of its name) and we were in the billet there. It was perhaps less than a week before we learned where we were going on OTU*, and that's where we would be going our separate ways.

## RAF Wellesbourne Mountford (September 1941)

Two of our little group were posted down to Wellesbourne Mountford for our OTU†. We were going to be doing the final bit of training

---

* Operational Training Unit
† This was No.22 OTU Wellesbourne Mountford 'C' Flight at the start, then 'B' Flight from end of September, and 'D' Flight from end of October

before we entered a squadron, and we were there for some time - with pilots, navigators, gunners, and wireless operator-gunners. We weren't 'crewed-up' at this stage - we trained alongside anyone, no matter what their role was.

When we arrived, we were met by an officer at the railway station, and of course it was clear from our uniforms we were all sergeants, except for this one chap. The officer said to him, 'Are you going aircrew?' 'Yes.' 'Why haven't you got your stripes on?' 'Because I haven't had time to...' Well, I don't think he was actually put on a 'Janker's call' as we called them, but he certainly got told off in front of the rest of us.

I remember that just before I left Manston, I wrote to Rudd and Smithy, my friends from Compton Bassett, to tell them I was going back to Yatesbury and no doubt they were already using the new Marconi. I wrote my name and station on the back, and sent the letters off. When I got down to Wellesbourne, I found my letter to Rudd had been returned to me, so I knew that something had happened to him, and I thought, 'Oh dear.' I didn't know what else to do about it. I knew he'd lived at Coggeshall in Essex, that's where he and his girlfriend used to get on (and sometimes at another station a little way up the line) when we were on weekend passes, but I couldn't remember her surname or address or anything like that. I knew that Rudd had been posted to a Halifax squadron somewhere in Yorkshire, but that's all I did know. I just had to assume he had gone... and I never heard anything from my other friend Smithy at all.

Jumping forward, much later, to 1945, I was at Gaydon then, an officer, and it was the end of the war, and I was being posted to 10 Group headquarters at Abingdon. While in a room there and looking for a scrap of paper to write on, I opened a cabinet up and there were some log books there, so I pulled one out and by sheer chance it was Rudd's, which had got mislaid from the time he left Yatesbury. He must have got another log book, as there was no entry in it after Yatesbury. I recognised the writing, his name and everything else, and I couldn't believe it.

Anyway, we started our air training at Wellesbourne in Wellington and Anson aircraft, doing our flying exercises while on the radio and so forth. It involved cross-country and night flights, 'circuits and bumps', the whole caboodle.

Then for part of our training, we were sent over to the satellite at RAF Atherstone, which was out a little further away from Stratford. While I was up there, I went with four others down to Stratford at the time they had their September fair - they had a name for it, I can't remember what.

There was one of these roundabouts that went up and down and I think there were three bench seats to each unit, something like that. These four other lads all got in the middle one, the back seat was already occupied, and the only spare space was in the front one - although there were two young schoolgirls already in there. I had to go in the front with them. The ride started up, and as it went faster and faster these girls, who were standing up, started to slide towards me. I thought heck, and in the end, they came right against me and ended up forcing me right out of the compartment as we went round. In fact, one of the girls was thrown out of the compartment with me. I cut my head, but she was all right. They stopped the roundabout (or whatever they called it) because of this.

I was taken off to the hospital to be seen to, and my four pals said, 'Right, we'll stay here and see you later on!' Well thanks very much! The two girls went off with me to the hospital, where I was sewn up and they put a big plaster on. After that, I went back into Stratford, met up with my four pals and went back to camp.

The next morning, I had to report to the sick bay. They said, 'Oh dear, now what happened to you?' When I told them, they laughed their heads off! I said, 'That's the truth...' and they said, 'All right, you won't be able to fly with that, so we'll see you in three or four days' time.'

So I thought, as I won't be called for flying, I think I'll go home. We were on a road that joined the London road eventually, so I thought, 'Righto, I'll hitch-hike.'

50

I got to the London road. There was a car with a young man and a young lady in, and he'd evidently borrowed his father's car. They were going back to London, so I got in the back, and off we went. Unfortunately, nearer London, when we were approaching some traffic lights, he didn't brake quite quickly enough and we went into the back of the car ahead. Not very severely, but of course that caused a bit of a hiccup. I thought, I'm not going to say anything about this at all. Luckily, I wasn't asked what had happened and I didn't have to make a statement. Anyway, they still got me from there into London, dropped me somewhere near a Tube station - so I made it to Liverpool Street and I went home, with this plaster on my head.

I walked in at home, and of course Mother thought I had been in an air crash first of all. I told her the truth, and even she said, 'Are you sure?' I said, 'Yes, I've not made it up, it's exactly what happened - and because I can't fly because of this, I thought I'd come home.' I had two or three days at home, and of course, down at Aldeburgh.

After returning to camp, I reported the following morning to the medical officer, and he said, 'All right, I think we can take that plaster off now, make it a little bit neater for you, and then you'll go back on flying duties.' So that's what happened - I managed to get a little bit of a break at that time (the end of September or beginning of October, I should think), otherwise I wouldn't have been home since the June.

We were given a leave of a week before we got posted to the squadron. I went home, and I met up with Dad in Ipswich - because he was working in Ipswich then. I met him at his lodgings at tea-time, I think it was, and it was there I told him I was going on the squadron. I said 'Now Dad, you do know what that means, don't you?' He said 'I do, but let me be the one who tells your mother. Don't you do it, I will.' I said 'All right, and Dad, I *shall* be all right.' Cocky I was, but anyway… I spent that week with Dorothy down at Aldeburgh and at Leiston, until I went back to Wellesbourne.

The OTU training at Wellesbourne went on until late November 1941, when we passed out from there, and I was posted to Coningsby in Lincolnshire.

51

### RAF Coningsby (December 1941)

Almost everyone on that course was being posted to Coningsby, to join 97 Squadron.

We had to get off the train at a place called Dogdyke. They'd told us there would be transport there waiting to take us to the RAF station, and there was, a WAAF* driver. They took us to camp, and we were put into the sergeant's mess, but it was full - in fact absolutely overcrowded. I forget now, but I shared a room with three or four others, I should think. We made up our beds and all the rest of it.

The next day when we reported down to the flight office, we found out that 97 Squadron was being re-formed. It had been flying in Avro Manchesters (the two-engined forerunner of the Lancaster), and that aircraft had a very bad reputation. They evidently lost more crews through crashes and so forth than they did on operations. However, they were still on Manchesters when we got there.

The squadron had a new Commanding Officer†, and he set to that day to crew us all up. We were in a large room and had to wait for our names to be called. We were getting towards the end of the session before this pilot came through, quite a big chap. He shouted out, 'Sergeant Grimwood?' 'Yes.' (Wireless operator.) 'Right, Sergeant Lancey?' 'Yes.' (Another pilot, Canadian). 'Right, Sergeant Smith?' 'Yes.' (Navigator, an Australian.) 'Sergeant Rouse?' (Gosh, that's me, second wireless operator and air gunner.) Then two more air gunners – Sergeants Humphrey (another Canadian) and Legace (a French-Canadian). Our pilot was David Maltby (he went on to become famous as a Dambusters pilot), George Lancey was second pilot and Maxie Smith our navigator. Eric Grimwood was first wireless operator and air gunner, and I was second. Lyle Humphrey was our tail gunner (and quite a lad - we always called him Humph), and Harvey Legace was mid-upper gunner - he stayed with us a while but not for all the time. So that was our seven, we were crewed-up.

---

* Women's Auxiliary Air Force
† This was Wing Commander Denys F.Balsdon

I think we had a trial flight in the Manchester just to get used to it, but about a week after that, we got aircrew leave. They used to send two crews off every week from the squadron on a week's leave, so it sort of rotated on a six weeks basis. It just happened that we got sent off on this particular week. So we got on the train, all the way down to London - Humph and the French-Canadian didn't, but David, Eric, Max, George and me all went together down to London. There we split up - because George, Maxie and possibly Eric were going to spend the time in London, Dave was going to his home (I think it was in Kent), and I was going back to Suffolk, obviously.

While on that leave, one day I was at home at Central Road, and over Mum's radio the news mentioned an air raid that had been taking place on the U-boat pens at a submarine base in France - a raid by Hampdens, Manchesters, and another aircraft I can't think of the name

*The crew, pictured in front of a Manchester aircraft they had trained in during early January 1942. Left to right, Harvey Legace, Lyle Humphrey, Max Smith, Eric Grimwood, Harold Rouse, George Lancey and David Maltby. This photograph was taken on the same occasion as the picture of Harold used centrally on the front cover of this book.*

of. And it was reported they'd suffered quite heavy casualties…. So I thought blimey, it must have been our squadron involved with that.

When we got back to camp, yes, it had been our squadron. Our CO* had been flying as a deputy - he had allowed another officer to be the pilot, but he wanted to go on the raid himself. He was in a Manchester which got badly shot up, but they did manage to make it back to Coningsby. As they came in to land, the controls broke, the plane went over on its back and they were all killed, right on their home base.

Two of them - the pilot, who was a Canadian, and the wireless operator, who was English - they were both buried in Coningsby churchyard. The CO was taken back to his home, the same for the other crew members. We had a funeral parade to attend, and we were detailed, not as pall-bearers, but to march beside the coffin down to the church in Coningsby. I remember the slow march first of all, then as we got away from the camp it was a quick march, then a slow march again as we arrived at the church. They took the coffins off, carried them in, we had the church service, and then those who were not going to be buried there were left in the church while they brought the other two out. We all had to go up to where the graves had been dug, and watch as they were put there.

So I thought, 'Oh blimey, this is operational life. But there you are, I've joined up, so I've got to get used to it.' It didn't put me off, it honestly didn't. Perhaps I just pushed it to the back of my mind, that was it.

Anyway, it was in the middle of January that we got called on the battle order. It turned out we were going to Hamburg in this Manchester bomber. There's a photograph of us all standing outside a Manchester, which I've got at home. So we had to get used to the routine - first we read up the briefing, then got briefed in person. We were going to take off early, because it was dark early in those days, and we were sent back to have our aircrew meal, the egg and all the

---

* Commanding Officer

54

rest of it - the traditional operational meal. It was then back to camp, to the airfield, and into the locker room where we got dressed up and equipped. As gunner, I was flying in the front turret. My first flying operation.

David had already done about fifteen operations in the Hampden aircraft with 106 Squadron – then he'd got transferred to 97, and so he'd done half a tour already. And Eric, the wireless operator, had also done a number of operations over there as well. The rest of us were rookies of course. But David, our experienced pilot, he was a marvellous skipper. As we were preparing to go, he said, 'All right chaps, I know what's going through your mind, but don't worry, I shall get you back!' I was grateful for that…

We got to the aircraft when it was time to get loaded up, and I had to sit down on the step beside the wireless operator for take-off - I wasn't allowed through to the front turret until we were airborne. As soon as we were, I went through, and off we went to Hamburg.

As you might expect, as we hit the enemy coast, there were searchlights, anti-aircraft fire and all that sort of thing. Over Hamburg, aircraft had already dropped some bombs and we did our own bombing run. Flying in that front turret was a most peculiar sensation because you felt you were entirely on your own, you were right out front in a ball flying through the air. You could hear the engines, but all the other crew members were way back there, out of sight.

There I was rotating the turret, when I saw the first of the flak (the anti-aircraft fire) coming up from the other side and I reported it to the captain. He said, 'OK, front gunner, I've seen it, OK,' and I thought well, he's experienced it before, so he must know what he's doing. And I was doing all the things a front gunner has to do - watching to make sure we weren't being caught by searchlights or by night fighters - although there weren't so many night fighting jobs in those days, fortunately.

Anyway, we got to Hamburg, dropped our load, which were all incendiaries if I remember rightly, and headed back. It was quite bad winter weather when we came back, and in the end, we had to do a bit of dog-legging to get through it. In the end, we arrived back to camp rather late, and we were getting a little low on petrol, or kerosene, the fuel. So David called up and advised the controller that we wanted to land as quickly as possible because we were getting low on fuel, so we were given priority. We landed safely with snow on the ground, all quite all right though, and that was it. David had got us back.

We went into debriefing, which was my first experience of that, cups of coffee with rum in, cigarettes of course, and giving our report to the various intelligence officers who were there. George reported on the bombing run - we didn't actually have a bomb aimer as such, but George, as the second pilot, did the bombing run and the bomb-aimer's job. And myself, well, I just sat around listening to the others, and didn't have to make much of a report - in fact I don't think I made any report at all.

It was then back to our billets, except for David who went back to his lodging in Woodhall Spa with his fiancée - I don't know if it was with relatives of hers, but she was living up there anyway. He'd managed to wangle a sleeping-out pass for that. We had to catch RAF vans back to Woodhall Spa, where we were billeted, as the camp at Coningsby was full up.

I was staying with a very elderly lady who lived with a companion who was suffering some sort of mental disturbance. Yes, she was a very posh lady, but she treated me very well. There were two others also staying there, from 106 Squadron, who'd been there for some time, but the first night I went in was the last night they were going to be there. My room was up in this attic lit by a candle, because there was no electricity up there. In the end, I was there for January and

*Australian crew-member Max Smith had never seen snow before, and is pictured here threatening a pilot (believed to be George Lancey) outside a hut at Coningsby*

*Five members of the crew in winter 1942, left to right:*
*George Lancey, Eric Grimwood, David Maltby, Max Smith,*
*Harold Rouse - in nonchalant mood, with pipe.*

February 1942. Then in March, when our Woodhall Spa aerodrome was finally completed (the accommodation and so forth), I moved into the billets on the station.

That first operation of mine took place on January 15th, which happened to be the anniversary of Louie's death two years earlier. I'd thought at the time, you know, 'Oh, is that an omen?' But it wasn't. And really and truly, for me, I was excited by the trip. I can honestly say I wasn't frightened, wasn't frightened at all - because I was just going into the unknown really, so that helped me I suppose.

So the next day, I thought, well, now I've done my first trip, I'll let Dad know. And silly, I shouldn't have done that really, but I thought what I'll do, I'll send him a telegram to where he was lodging. I'll just put on it 'NUMBER ONE COMPLETED, EVERYTHING OK.

57

*This studio portrait is dated 17th January 1942 on the back - just two days after Harold's first operational mission.*

LOVE HAROLD.' Whether that gave him a fright when he first picked it up, I didn't think that way - I just wanted to let them know I'd got over number one.

I didn't send one to Dorothy, but afterwards I wrote a letter to tell her I'd been operating, because I used to write to her every day. I just used to tell her I was flying last night - I didn't say where or anything like that - some of it was training flights anyway. So she never knew where I was going - except maybe once, on my fifth operation, which I may have mentioned to her...

### RAF Woodhall Spa (April 1942)

After that first op in January 1942, February and March were mostly taken up transferring over to the Lancasters really. At the same time, I moved out of my accommodation into the huts at the new aerodrome at Woodhall Spa, and carried on from there.[*]

In the last week of March and into April, I was sent on a week-long gunnery course, at Scampton I think it was, with others[†]. This was an advanced course, flying with camera guns mounted on the aircraft, and with Spitfires coming in to invade us.

We got to the end of that week, on the Friday I think it was, and they said, 'Right, that's the end of the course, now we'll give you all

---

[*] The locations in Harold's log book in March and April are recorded as 'Tattershall Thorpe', then from May as 'Woodhall Spa'

[†] This is shown in Harold's log book as 'GTF Scampton' (Gunnery Training Flight)

*Typical scene at Woodhall Spa aerodrome, 1942*

your marks.' They handed out the marks to us individually without saying what they were. And then the instructor said, 'Right, anyone who got 100 per cent?' No. 'Anyone got 95 per cent?' No. 'Well, anyone over 90?' I put my hand up, I'd got 93. And I was the only one. He said, 'Right, you're the top of the class.' Well, thanks very much. And he said, 'That means you can go off for the weekend, this weekend.' I said, 'Well, do you think it can be changed to next weekend for me?' I told them it was because it was coming up to my twenty-first birthday, and I'd like to get home for that. He said, 'All right, we'll arrange with your squadron to have *next* weekend.' I said thanks very much indeed.

I went back with the others to Woodhall Spa, and it was about three days later, that I had my first operation on the Lancaster - four days before my birthday.

I was in the front turret again, this time on a job to drop mines - we called those 'gardening' jobs - off one of the islands in the North Sea that the Germans were occupying. It was quite a simple exercise really. The only thing we had to watch out for was gunships, in case they were about. We laid our mines, came back, and that was that. It was the Wednesday night, 8th April 1942.

Once again, I hadn't had the chance to tell them I was coming home for the weekend - I came home unexpectedly. I found brother Bertie and his Dorothy (who hadn't yet got married at that stage) already at Central Road, Leiston. My Dorothy was also staying there for the weekend, but when I got in off the train, she wasn't there - she'd gone up to the local school for a dance. So Bertie and Dorothy said 'Come on, have something to eat and drink, then we'll all go up.' So we did, into my old school up on the Saxmundham Road. I walked in, and of course gave her the surprise of her life. She'd been dancing with this young soldier and stopped dead as soon as she saw me, sort of leaving him in the middle of the floor.

I said 'Look, go back and finish your dance and then we'll take it from there.' We spent the evening finishing off the dance and then walked home. Quite what the sleeping arrangements must have been in the house at Central Road I haven't the foggiest idea. I think the two Dorothys slept together in the middle bedroom, Mum and Dad were in the front bedroom, Bertie had the little bedroom and I think I must have slept on the settee downstairs. That's the only way we could have arranged it I think, something like that anyway.

The Sunday was my birthday. After breakfast, Dorothy and Bertie, Dot and I decided to walk down to Aldringham. It was a beautiful morning and the sun was shining, it was warm and very nice indeed. We got down to the Parrot and Punchbowl, the hostelry there, we went in and had a drink, then we walked back for lunch at home.

As before, I think I took Dorothy back to Aldeburgh in the evening on the Sunday, because she would be having to go back to work on the Monday morning. I must have slept at hers at Victoria Road at Aldeburgh that night, possibly on the settee in the other room. All the concern about these sleeping arrangements seems odd these days - but they weren't straightforward at all! Anyway, I left on the Monday to go back to the squadron.

One evening, soon after we'd moved into the huts at Woodhall Spa, George and Max, Eric and I thought we'll go out for the night, we'll walk into Boston. It was quite a way there, so we got a lift in an RAF truck to start with. We got to Boston, which it was reputed had - not quite a pub for every day of the year, like Norwich - but quite a lot of pubs.

We said right, we'll have a drink in every pub. So we started off. Well, George was not really a drinker, and he kept to shandy. Max and myself, we had bitter and I think Eric did as well - it wasn't very strong bitter anyway. I think we visited about eight pubs that night, but that was all, we couldn't manage any more. We then caught the transport back to camp, and that was it.

A bit later on, a few weeks afterwards, we heard there was a dance going on down at Boston, in the hall in the centre of the town, and I went down, not with Eric, but with someone else in the squadron. That was the occasion when I first met Peggy Harrison and her parents, who I got to know well during the rest of 1942 - I'll describe that in a bit more detail later.

# PART III: Theatre of war

## More operational action (April 1942)

Soon after that, there was a bit of a flap on - we were all training for this, that and the other - getting ready, although none of us knew it at the time, for the Augsburg daylight raid.

Six aircraft from 97 Squadron had been chosen along with two reserves, but the rest of us in the squadron weren't actually on the battle list. That was on April 17th, I think. The six Lancasters went flying off, together with the two reserves needed in case there was any hold-up, on this raid to Augsburg in daylight.

The other squadron that had converted to Lancasters at the same time as us, 44 Squadron, they'd also sent six aircraft. Well, they lost aircraft soon after they'd hit the enemy coast. There was a German fighter squadron on a training flight, and when they suddenly saw Lancasters, of course they pounced on them. Only two of the RAF planes got out of that fight to carry on to Augsburg. And then one of those got lost over the target. Only the one survived, under Squadron Leader Nettleton, who led the flight. He got the VC, I might add.

Our six aircraft, under Squadron Leader Sherwood, well they took a slightly different route over the continent. They were luckier than the other group. All six of them made it to the target, and they were dropping 11 second delayed bombs - so two went in, dropped the bombs, it was 11 seconds before the bombs went off, and then the next two went in, and so forth.

Well, Sherwood led the first two in, got badly hit and managed to drop his bomb but subsequently crashed, and in fact, he was the only one of his crew who came out of it alive - he was made a prisoner of war at the end. The next one got badly shot up, I can't remember who

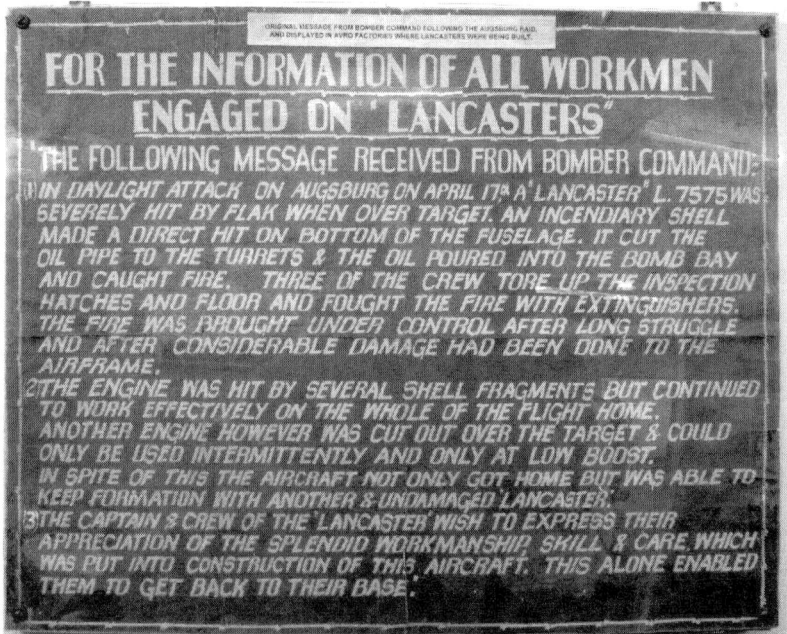

*Sign originally displayed in Lancaster factory following the Augsburg raid in April 1942 – and now in Thorpe Camp aviation museum.*

that was, but they carried on. And then the next two went in, one of them was piloted by a Warrant Officer, and he got shot up and crashed.

So we did lose two on the target. But the other four all made it back eventually, badly holed and so forth. On one of those, they had a bad fire on board which one of my fellow wireless operators, Ron Irons, managed to put out - he got the DFM* because of that.

## Tirpitz raids (April 1942)

Well, a week after that, on Friday 24th April, our crew having been on non-requirements for the Augsburg raid, we were sent up to RAF Lossiemouth in Scotland - but we didn't know what for. We simply

---

* Distinguished Flying Medal

had to go up to Lossiemouth and land there. When we got there, there were some other Lancasters from another squadron, and a squadron of Halifaxes as well. On the Saturday, we were sitting there at Lossiemouth but we were told we wouldn't be going on the operation that night because the weather wasn't suitable, and the same again happened on the Sunday.

On that Sunday night, Dave our skipper said, 'Well, as we're not going out tonight either, let's go down into Elgin and see if we can get a drink.' But of course, Scotland didn't have any drinking on Sundays. Anyway, five of us went down - there was David, George, Max, Eric and myself - we all walked into the town. We found this pub and the door was closed, but we could hear voices inside. We knocked on the door, someone came to the door, and we said, 'Oh, we wondered if we can get a drink?' 'Of course, you're travellers, you can come in!'

So they took us in, and we had a few drinks in there, and quite a nice evening. We came out afterwards and went back to the bus stop where we wanted a bus back to Lossiemouth. While standing at the bus stop, we four, all sergeants, thought we'd stand David, a flying officer, on his head! Which we did. Just as we did that, two military police came up, and said 'Right, we're putting you on a charge.' David got up off the floor where we had dropped him and he said in a loud voice, 'Bugger off. This is my crew and if they want to stand me on my head they can do so! Go, now go!' So they left us, and we went back to Lossiemouth.

On Monday 27th April we got the briefing. We were going up to Trondheim in Norway, after the *Tirpitz*, the German battleship which was moored there.

We took off at dusk-time and flew across the North Sea. It was a brilliant moonlit night - you could see for miles. It was quite a long trip across up there of course, but we hit the coast at Norway and found our way to the Trondheim Fjord. We could see the *Tirpitz* moored up: we looked right down at the ship tight against its mooring as we came in at an angle. At the edge of the fjord there were huge cliffs coming up steeply. At first, we thought, oh blimey, but as we were going in at 6,000 or 8,000 feet, we knew we'd be all right for those cliffs there.

*Lancaster R5495, in which Harold flew for both the Tirpitz raids. This aircraft was later shot down over Essen in June 1942.*

I was in the front turret and I thought I'd need to keep a good view of this, so I turned my guns up, and took my hands off the controls. George was down in the bomb aimer's position ready to drop the bombs. The skipper had already opened the bomb doors and we were making our run in. I think it was a 4,000 lb bomb we were dropping that night and also some 500 lb ones.

As we were going along, suddenly my guns started firing off on their own - they were shooting up in the air! Evidently, what had happened was that the firing gear, which was a bit like the cable brakes on a bicycle, had got caught on what they called the back plate - which pulled it, and set the guns off. There were shells going everywhere. So we had to do a dummy run and go round again, which we did. Our squadron actually lost one aircraft that night, and I got blamed for shooting it down - I hope in jest, but that's not the point. And it wasn't my fault - he shouldn't have been up at that height anyway.

So we went in on the second run, by which time the Germans had got wise to us and started their smoke screens, but we could still

see where the *Tirpitz* was, and George dropped the bomb. We got over the cliffs, turned round, came out and that was it. Then a nice journey back over the North Sea, once again in a brilliant

*Extract from reconnaissance photograph supplied to 97 Squadron before the raid in April 1942*

moonlit night. I remember seeing a British frigate/warship on patrol down there as we went over. And we got back to Lossiemouth. I think the whole trip took 8 or 8½ hours, something like that - I can soon look that up in my log book.

Funnily enough, that was the same night that Norwich got the Blitz - Monday 27th April. I didn't know about that until I heard it on the radio - they didn't specifically mention Norwich, but I heard that several places on the East Coast had been bombed that night.

On the Tuesday, we got briefed again to go after the *Tirpitz* - because evidently, they hadn't made the hits that they wanted to make the damage complete. So we were sent off to do the same sort of trip all over again, which we did.

This time when we got there, the smoke screen over the *Tirpitz* had been put up early, but we had been given an alternative target to drop some of our bombs on - I think it was a German warship in another fjord a little way away. We went after that. They'd put a smoke screen up but it wasn't very effective, so we bombed on that that night, then we came back. Once again, brilliant moonlight, and it was a marvellous trip when you think about it. We got back to Lossiemouth in the early hours of Wednesday morning.

And after we had got up on Wednesday morning and had breakfast, or a late meal whatever it was, we were told that we were being sent back to our squadron base.

As we all got in our Lancaster, Dave said, 'Right, we're going from this place now, so we're going to do a beat-up on the aerodrome.' I said 'Right, shall I get in the front turret for you?' 'Yes,' he said, 'I'll give you word when you can come in the front turret.'

We took off, we went round and he said, 'Right, get in the front turret,' so I went through. He then came down very low and flew the Lancaster right between two of the hangars. And all the rest of the squadron were doing the same thing, a real beat-up, you know. Just to show off, really and truly. Then we left and got back to Woodhall Spa sometime in the afternoon, and that was it, my fourth trip.

## Lucky landing (May 1942)

My next trip came about on May 4th. We were going to Stuttgart. And we were going to be crossing over the coast at Aldeburgh. I thought, now that's rather interesting, and I admit I may have quietly let a certain someone know we were likely to be flying overhead that night.

I was in the front turret again. It was dark when we took off if I remember rightly, and it was still dark when we crossed over the coast, but anyway I could see when we did so. I thought, 'Well Dorothy, you're down there somewhere, and I'm up here.'

Half an hour later we hit the enemy coast, and that's where we got rather badly hit up. We lost our hydraulics - we couldn't open the bomb doors, and the wheels came down but they weren't locked.

Dave said we're in a bit of a state and we can't carry on, so we'll have to go back. We flew along the coast to see whether we could get rid of our bombs, because we had 3,304 incendiary bombs on board. They were in 14 cases in our bomb bay - they were small magnesium bombs really, 236 in a case. So we were carrying quite a big bomb load - I suppose it was over six tons. But we couldn't get rid of them because we couldn't open the bomb doors.

We turned round to come back. I think we crossed over somewhere near Norwich to go up to the Wash and then we got back to Woodhall Spa. David called up and they said, 'Well, you better land at Coningsby,' which was still a grass aerodrome - Woodhall Spa being concrete. He said, 'All right,' and we went round to Coningsby and got permission from there to land.

We touched down onto the grass, we bounced, bounced once again but just couldn't slow down enough. The runway finished up near a corner and there was a gun emplacement there, and as we tore along, they all jumped out of the gun emplacement. We crossed over one road, a field, another road and then into another field, and finally ended up with our nose against a tree. Fortunately, as no front gunner was allowed in the front turret during landing, I'd already got out from there - just as well, because my front turret was absolutely mangled.

*Photos taken by Eric Grimwood of the crash site at Coningsby on the morning after – 5th May 1942. Inset left, George Lancey and Dave Maltby sitting back in the cockpit. Lower right, forward view out along the fuselage past the wireless post.*

It was about half past two in the morning. There was a farm cottage not far away, and people came running out of there because they had heard us come down. But we all managed to get out of the aircraft. I think George bumped his head. David, who was a broad chap, he told us he escaped through his side window - it seemed hardly wide enough for him to go through, but he went through. I think our gunner Legace also got a bit of a bump - he'd got out of his turret by then of course. But we were all quite safe.

And the aircraft didn't go up, neither did the bombs fortunately. The fire engine and an ambulance and all the rest of it turned up from the station, took us back to the mess, we had our flying breakfast, our egg again, and went off to bed.

The next morning, the five of us (David, George, Max, Eric and myself) went and viewed our aircraft. As I said previously, David was living out at Woodhall Spa with his fiancée at some relatives or friends of hers, and he had the use of their car. So he drove to the station and picked us four up, and we went and viewed the wrecked aircraft in daylight. It had been brand-new just the previous day. S for sugar (we didn't call it S for sugar though)[*].

It had broken its back, one wheel was here and another wheel was there, the nose was right up against this tree. Eric took some photographs, and later, after Eric was lost, I found them amongst his belongings, and I thought, 'I'm going to have these.'

Since then, someone asked to see those pictures at Connie's, and I think I must have forgotten that I'd left them with her, and I never did get them back - at least I can't trace them anywhere. Anyway, I know we did get a photograph of our crash-landed aircraft at the time before it was all cleared away.

---

[*] All squadron planes were given an alphabetic identifier and call-sign (those flown in by Harold Rouse throughout 1942 are listed in the table in Appendix 5)

69

*Dave Maltby (centre) inspects the wreck along with two others (one of whom is probably George Lancey, but could be Harold Rouse)*

---

*As it happened, those photographs did turn up amongst Harold's family snaps - they were not lost after all. They give a fascinating glimpse of the written-off aeroplane taken just as the ground crew were in the process of removing it. The set of nine small prints includes a shot of Dave Maltby and others in discussion as they took a close look at the wreckage, just a few hours after they had got out of the plane alive.*

*There are very few clues in these pictures as to the precise location of the crash site, only a tree, a nearby road and a distant view of a building. But together with Harold's description of bouncing across two roads beyond the end of the runway, it has been possible to narrow it down to one of two locations beyond the edge of the then airfield (one of these possible locations has since been covered by an eastward extension of the main runway).*

---

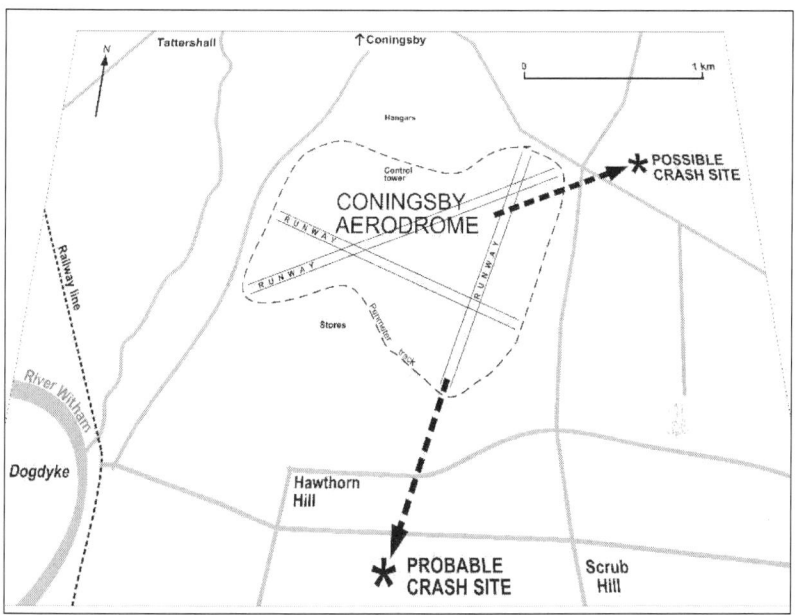

*Sketch map showing possible locations of the crash-landing
of Lancaster R5553 on 5th May 1942*

*Modern view westwards along the road from Scrub Hill towards Dogdyke
showing the probable crash location south of Coningsby Aerodrome*

### Gunner to main wireless operator (May 1942)

That crash-landing was how my fifth trip ended, and it was the last operation where I was in the front turret. Because after that, Eric said

*Lancaster interior mock-up showing wireless operator at work, a display at Thorpe Camp Museum. You can see the similar forward view along the fuselage amongst the crash photos.*

he was going to re-muster as a bomb-aimer, so he left and I got detailed as the wireless operator on the crew. So we carried on. Someone else came in - we must have had another gunner at the front I think, just temporarily. There wasn't any other wireless operator, I know that.

Anyway, I did another six or so trips with David before the end of May - they must all be listed in my log book.

---

*Harold did not include any specific description here of his remaining six trips with David Maltby as captain, although of course, they are detailed in the log book[\*]. They are listed as his raid nos. 6-11 on the operations map towards the back of this book[†]. They included 'gardening' (mine-laying) operations off Kiel, Copenhagen and elsewhere in the Baltic, and bombing raids to industrial targets deep in Germany, at Warnemünde and at Mannheim, where the Heinkel aircraft factory was located.*

*Although these journeys were recorded as uneventful for the most part, they were certainly not without extreme potential danger. On*

---

[\*] See extracts from his log book in Appendix 4
[†] See the list of raids on the map in Appendix 7

*several occasions, the Lancasters they were flying in were caught in searchlights and flak, one being recorded as holed in both the rudder and wheel nacelle while over Germany, and another damaged after an accurate heavy anti-aircraft shell exploded just under the nose of the aeroplane during one of the Baltic trips.*

*Model of Lancaster L7571, in which Harold's crew flew their sixth mission to Kiel in early May 1942, two days after their crash-landing. This model is part of a display at Thorpe Camp Museum. This aircraft had successfully reached Stuttgart on that night with a different crew. It was subsequently shot down in September 1942.*

### David's departure (May 1942)

On the 29th of May, David Maltby suddenly said to us, 'Chaps, I've got leave for next week.' We said, 'But we haven't got any leave.' He said, 'No, but as you know, I'm engaged, and they've given me special leave to go and get married – tomorrow, in fact.' On Saturday 30th, I think it was. All we could say was, 'All right, fair enough.'

Well that Saturday, we learned that the whole squadron was on standby. And in fact, it turned out it was going to be the 'thousand-bomber raid' that was starting that night. Aircraft came from all over the country - some crews still on training exercises, some which had done ops but come back from rest, and so forth.

George and Max were sent over to Coningsby to make up two other crews over there. But Eric and myself, Humph and our French-

Canadian gunner Legace, we were left without a captain, and weren't required at all. We were the only ones that didn't go out from our squadron on the thousand-bomber raid. It wasn't until the next morning that we knew what was going on. As it turned out, the losses on that raid were fortunately quite small - our squadron didn't lose any aircraft, anyway.

*Extract from an official 97 Squadron photograph, taken at Woodhall Spa in May 1942. David Maltby is seated in the centre of this view, with Harold standing behind his right shoulder.*

Following that, we were told that David wouldn't be coming back for the end of the week. We then heard a whisper he was being sent on a rest, meaning that he wouldn't be doing any more ops for the time being. George was told in a further instruction that he would be taking over as captain of our aircrew. But for the time being, around the beginning of June, we were just doing anything that was wanted on the squadron - a little bit of training flying, but not much more.

**Short interlude** (June/July 1942)

I then got posted along with eleven others, not just from my squadron but from other squadrons as well, to Great Malvern on a TRE (telecommunications research establishment) course. This was housed in the girls' school at Great Malvern.

We got down there, and we were put in billets in a big house overlooking the green at Great Malvern. There were four of us in one room, four others in the room beneath us, and more elsewhere in the building. On the first day, we reported in to the college and sat down to have this first lecture. It turned out they'd also sent a lot of ground crew on the same course, wireless mechanics and so forth.

Well, before long, we were starting to think we'd been put into a school of mad scientists - that's really what those running the course looked like, and also what they sounded like. This chap started off, and after about three words, we were absolutely lost, what with all the technicalities that came out...

The sum total of this course appeared to be that they were trying to develop a bomb release system without a bombsight, and it was to be done using electronic gear with traffic lights which the wireless operator would have to operate. I thought blimey, this is going to be peculiar.

Anyway, they went into the technical side so deeply and it was so incomprehensible to us aircrew, we decided that we wouldn't trouble to go in to the course any more. In the days that followed, we instead went down to the local pub and sat in the sun. We probably didn't lose anything by it, because we couldn't do any practical flying, and we couldn't understand the theory. The people of Great Malvern, who I don't think had seen aircrew before then, treated us very well. They gave us a free dinner one night in one of the pubs, I remember. That was quite nice. From memory, we were there about three weeks.

Then we went back to squadron and no sooner had we got there than we were told, 'Right, you're going off RAF Silloth now - it's in Cumberland.' It was to do some air flying with this new-fangled equipment. I wrote a quick note to Dorothy saying, 'Right, I'm off Scotland way [I didn't say exactly where], and I'll let you know later on.' So off we went again on the train - up to Newcastle, then via Carlisle to Silloth.

They were flying American planes there, small planes, and in fact there were only two of us aircrew who would be able to do any flying in them at any one time. They explained they didn't have enough aircraft serviceable, that was the reason. I think it was a fortnight we were up there, and in the end, we never did fly once. I'd drawn a parachute in readiness at the parachute section.

One morning as we got up, word went round that an aircraft was coming from Coningsby to pick up certain people to take them back. So we said we may as well go back with them. I remember that I hadn't time to go to the parachute section to book my parachute in, so I said to one chap that was in the billet, 'Look, will you put this in for me?', which he agreed to do. I dashed off, got into the aircraft, with all of us sitting in the fuselage, and they took us to Coningsby. Then we had to leg it back to our base at Woodhall Spa - thankfully, it wasn't too far.

As soon as we got back, the first thing we said to the CO was to request a 48-hour pass. He said, 'All right, since we're not ready for you yet.' So we got our passes, and off I went home again.

That was the time that I turned up back in Aldeburgh with no advanced notice, and found Dorothy in the cinema with that army sergeant she had met before. I knew the cashier and the usherette at the cinema, and I said, 'I believe Dorothy is in the cinema,' and the usherette said, 'Yes, she is.' I said, 'Is there any chance of me having a seat?' She said, 'Yes, all right.' I went to the cash desk, and the cashier said, 'Yes, she's not gone.' So the usherette took me across the cinema up there to the back row. The seats at the beginning of that row were empty, and Dorothy and the army sergeant and a few others were there, but all the seats next to Dorothy were empty. So I got in, sat down next to her and said, 'Good evening.' I think if the floor had opened up, I would have gone down there myself with her.

I can't remember what the film was, but it was about halfway through by the time I got in there. Anyway, we came out of the cinema and the sergeant said, 'Let's go off to the sergeant's mess and have a drink.' 'Oh, very nice of you,' I said, 'Thanks very much.' He took us off to the mess, which was at the foot of Church Hill in Aldeburgh. Then the two of us left him and walked back to Dorothy's home at Victoria Road. I had Saturday night and Sunday night there, and then had to go back to squadron on the Monday.

So that was another unexpected visit home. Normally we got just one week's leave every six weeks, and weekend passes were unheard of really. But I was lucky enough to get two quite quickly, one in April and one in June.

---

*Harold mentions next to nothing about the ongoing losses suffered by 97 Squadron, but he later marked up an official squadron photograph with a small black cross placed against all those colleagues and acquaintances who he knew had been killed or missing during operations or in flying accidents - and it was a considerable number.*

*One loss which must have deeply affected him at this time was that of his friend and former crew-mate Sgt Eric Grimwood, a fellow wireless operator who had stepped aside in May (after Harold's fifth operation), having decided to re-muster as a bomb aimer. Eric's move meant Harold took over the wireless operator's seat in the Lancaster instead of being in the front gun turret.*

*Eric had already flown a number of missions in the same crew as David Maltby in 1941 before the latter formed his own aircrew with Eric and Harold as fellow members. After re-mustering, Eric joined a Lancaster aircrew under Flying Officer McMurchy from mid-June, and flew eleven more operations. On 26th July 1942, they were reported missing during a mission to Hamburg. This was just five days before Harold resumed intensive flying operations after his own nine-week interlude.*

*On an occasion prior to the recording on which this transcript is based, Harold had told of the agonising job he had of breaking the news to Eric's mother (believed to be a widow) that her 20-year-old son Eric was missing and presumed dead. It is evident that Harold had the responsibility for collecting and returning Eric's possessions, amongst which were the photographs Eric had taken of the scene of their crash-landing in May. It is those pictures Harold decided to hang onto (and are reproduced in this book on pages 68 and 70).*

---

**Action recommences** (August 1942)

The rest of June and July was taken up with training work on the Lancaster, and I think our next operation was in August. I can't remember now the exact date or where to, but it was the first one when George Lancey took over as captain and I was the wireless operator.[*]

And things carried on like that for the rest of 1942 - doing ops mostly by night, and occasionally flying two nights on the trot. George was our pilot for all of those.

We did a number of raids through September, October and into November, including a couple of times flying all the way to Italy. On one of those long trips across the Alps, we'd done the bombing and were on our way back, and I remember looking up and there was a clear sky. I said, 'Ah, there's our stars - the Little Bear'. Dorothy and I always called them our stars,

*The Italian port of Genoa lit up by RAF flares, late 1942. Harold flew there in October and November*

---

[*] This was a successful raid on Kassel in Germany on 27th August

and I saw them quite clearly. I used to take her photograph along with me, and I used to say, 'Look, our stars are up there...' I thought that's nice to know anyway...

We got into December, and on December 8<sup>th</sup> I think it was, we were given another trip to northern Italy. When I got back, it was coming up to Christmas and there wasn't much flying going on.

*Lancaster R5497 pictured in action over France during the low-level raid to Le Creusot in October 1942. Harold was in a different aeroplane that night, but flew in this particular aircraft (OF-Z) on three other raids that year, before it was shot down in mid-December.*

*Once again, you'll notice how little Harold says about these further seventeen dangerous flight operations, as numbered 12 to 28 on the map in Appendix 7. They were typically delivering 4-5,000 lb bombloads, incendiaries or mines on long-distance missions necessitating between 5 and 9 hours in the air to complete each round trip - much of it over enemy territory at night-time.*

*On three of those sixteen missions, they were forced to turn back before reaching the target: once because of serious flak damage en route, once because of electrical problems, and once because they just couldn't keep up with a large formation of allied bombers. These were flying from the Bay of Biscay to Le Creusot in France on a surprise daytime raid code-named Operation Robinson.*

*Official notes made during the captain's debriefing from the trips refer to occasional problems caused by heavy flak or searchlights, bad weather, thick smoke, and towards the end of November, an increasing risk of night fighters. On the journey to Nurnberg on 28<sup>th</sup> August, they* *had to turn very promptly for home after dropping four 2,000 lb bombs, because of the realisation that they had used up more fuel than expected in getting to the target. On the long trip to Turin on 28th November, George Lancey recorded seeing the glow from many fires visible from the Alps, on both the way there and back.*

*The crew had always been allocated various different Lancaster aircraft, both on these raids and for non-combat flights, so it seems they were not given any option of choosing the aircrew's favourite or 'lucky' aircraft.*

*Appendix 5 includes a table listing the identification numbers of all the aircraft Harold flew in during 1942, whether for training, air tests or combat missions, and the final fate of those aeroplanes where known.*

*Of the 27 different aircraft recorded, all but five had either been shot down or crashed by the end of 1944. In some cases, the planes were lost only a matter of days after Harold had flown in them, and of course in one particular case (R5553), he was still on board when the aircraft was written off in a crash-landing in May 1942, as already described on pages 67-71.*

*Lancaster R5609, another aircraft Harold flew in for training in September and October 1942. Its OF-S designation was taken over from the plane written off in their May crash-landing.*

80

## The Harrisons

I mentioned before how a few of us from the squadron had one day taken a bus down to Boston to go to a dance, sometime in late Spring 1942. Well, on that occasion, a little time after arriving, I was looking around for a dance partner and I saw a young lady standing with a man and a woman. I thought they looked like her parents.

Anyway, I thought she seemed to be looking for a dance, so I went up and asked if I could have a dance. She said yes, and I learnt it was indeed her parents with her, who also gave their permission. So we danced, and I found out her name was Peggy Harrison. She had a sister and a brother who were twins, and her brother Ray was in the RAF, a ground staff. Her father was a master baker in a cake shop in Boston.

I think Peggy had just celebrated her eighteenth birthday, but I've never been certain of that, to be quite honest. Anyway, that would explain why her mother and father brought her out to the dance, if it was the very first time.

Anyway, before I said goodnight to them and went back to camp, her mother had said to me, 'Would you like to come to tea tomorrow?' I said that's very kind, but I didn't know whether I shall be on duty. 'Well,' she said, 'We live at Hospital Lane. Your bus comes down the Horncastle Road beside the river, and it will stop at a bridge. If you come over that bridge, you'll be in Hospital Lane, and we're number 32 a little way along on the left.' So I said that's very kind of you, and thank you very much.

On the Sunday, I wasn't flying or anything like that, so I caught the bus down to Boston. Peggy was waiting to see me off the bus and took me to her home. We had tea, and after that her parents said, 'Well, we were thinking we'd like to go out for a drink - we wonder, would you like to come with us?' I said thank you, and so we went out and had a drink. Of course, I then I had to go back to camp. I think the last bus up there went at about half past nine, so I couldn't stay very late.

*Modern view of the junction between Horncastle Road (left) and the bridge at Hospital Lane (right) in Boston, where Harold got off the bus when visiting the Harrisons. Their house is visible in the far distance over the bridge.*

And so they took me in rather like a son, and to be quite honest, I looked upon Peggy as a younger sister. In the end, I used to go down to them virtually every night when I wasn't on duty during 1942.

We only went to dances, as Peggy wasn't keen on the cinema. But one night I did want to go to the cinema. It was to see *Dangerous Moonlight* - I remember it quite well with the Warsaw concerto – I'd wanted to see that. But the dance was also on. So I suggested that she went to the dance, and I went to the cinema. 'Now if you meet anyone there who wants to walk you home, don't worry, I'll follow on – it's just your mother and father will be expecting me to get you home. I'll come over to the dance when I come out of the cinema.' Which I did, and as it happened, she hadn't met anyone else, so I walked home with her as usual.

Peggy's mother always waited up to see us in after the dance. It finished at a quarter to twelve, so by twelve o'clock, we were usually back in number 32. We used to have a cup of tea for supper, and because it was so late, they let me stay overnight, as I could catch the early bus in the morning. They made up a bed for me in the other room on the sofa, and I slept there, which was very kind of them.

The station wouldn't allow us to go away on leave that Christmas, but I was allowed to go off camp locally. They said, 'All right, if you're going to go into Boston, we can get hold of you if we want you.' So I gave them the address where I'd be. In this way I spent Christmas with Peggy, her sister Betty, her mother and father. Peggy's brother wasn't home on leave that Christmas, neither was Betty's boyfriend - he was wherever Ray was, as they were both in the RAF. I was treated very well, like a member of the family. I shared in their Christmas meal, had a drink with them at the local hostelry in the evening, and when we got home, we had a cup of tea, before we all went off to our respective beds.

## End of tour (December 1942)

I caught the bus back to camp the next morning, Boxing Day, and found that everything was still all right at Woodhall Spa. So I went back down to Boston again on the bus later that day for another night at the Harrisons.

The day after that, back I went again to camp, and this time they said to me, 'Oh, you've finished your tour, you're going on a rest now.'

I was told I was being posted back to Wellesbourne in Warwickshire. And I was to go there on the 28th December, I think it was. That meant I had to spend the day of the 27th back at camp going through all the sections getting checked out and signed off for this, that and the other. It was quite a rigmarole, returning all the things we were not allowed to keep, all that sort of thing.

And then on the following day, I had just enough time to go down to Boston and say to the Harrisons, 'Right, well, I've finished here, I'm now being posted to Warwickshire, I'll give you an address when I get there,' and that was it, that was sort of goodbye.

# PART IV: Recalibration

## Wellesbourne Mountford again (January 1943)

Off I went, back to Wellesbourne[*] along with one other chap from the squadron. After I got there, the first thing they did was to give us a week's leave...which was very handy.

Wellesbourne was where I had previously done my OTU, but this time I was going to be there as a 'screener'. This was not exactly instructing, but supervising the pupils in the air, always in the air rather than on the ground. It wasn't while they were doing circuits and landings, 'circuits and bumps' as we used to call them, but when they did cross-country, that's when we went with them. We did air tests with the pilots, mostly in Wellington aircraft. The pilot always had to take a wireless operator while on an air test. Yes, that was quite fun.

Going back a moment, I could have mentioned that while I was at Woodhall Spa in a hut there, I'd had a radio set. I'd taken the radio which we'd had at home, quite a small one, running off the mains, and had it in my room there, with an aerial outside and an earth wire going out of the window, so I could hear the news as it was. Well, I didn't want to carry that to Wellesbourne, so when I'd gone down to the Harrisons for the last time, I'd taken it with me and asked Mrs Harrison if she minded if I left it there. She said 'Of course not, come back and fetch it whenever you like.' I said right, thank you.

Well, when we got to Wellesbourne and they said we could have a week's leave, of course I went back home to Suffolk. That ran into the New Year, and for some reason I found out I could only get to Boston on New Year's Eve. So I said to Dorothy, 'Look, I want to go and pick this radio up - I don't want to leave it there too long.' She

---

[*] This was No.22 Operational Training Unit Wellesbourne

said, all right, but you don't want to miss New Year. I agreed, but she said it would be all right to go.

So off I went to Boston on New Year's Eve. Now there happened to be a dance there that night, and Ray, Peggy's brother, and his pal who was fiancé to Betty, we all went to the dance. And I don't mind admitting that during that dance, my mind was not on Peggy, but on Dorothy, while I was dancing. In fact, I thought, 'Oh dear, she's there in Aldeburgh and I'm here, we ought to be together.' It was obviously a bit awkward when later I realised Peggy may have got the wrong impression. Anyway, I did get back home to Dorothy the following day, as I still had two days' leave, then after that I returned to Wellesbourne.

## RAF Gaydon (January 1943)

I had only been at Wellesbourne about a fortnight when I was then posted over to Gaydon, the satellite to Wellesbourne.

The job there was to fly with the young chaps doing OTU, as we had done ourselves originally, sort of supervising them, and so forth. I was in 'B' Flight with some of the others who were in 97 Squadron, so we already knew each other.

*Unlabelled photograph from Harold's collection, thought to have been taken at Gaydon in winter 1943, with a Wellington aircraft behind. Harold is seated on the extreme right-hand end (see extract overleaf)*

*Extract from photograph on previous page, thought to be at Gaydon*

We were billeted in a Nissen hut, but oh dear, it was a terrible place - in the wintertime it was deadly cold, and in the summertime, it was too hot. But anyway, that was that. It was at Gaydon that I got my promotion to Flight Sergeant.

Occasionally I was able to get a weekend off to go home, and then every twelve weeks I got a proper week's leave. Now Dorothy's sister Gwen and Bill were going to get married on February 13th in 1943, and Bill had previously asked me whether I'd be his best man. I'd said I would if I can get leave. And fortunately, the leave came up just at that time.

So I was able to go home and be best man to Bill at that wedding, which they had at Aldeburgh Church. For the reception, all the neighbours had got their rations together, and one of them next door to Dorothy's had made a nice cake for them.

The reception was held at the British Legion hut on the steps at Aldeburgh.* It was the only place that was available, as the army had taken over everything else.

I remember that night after things had finished, we all went back to the house at Victoria Road. It was on the Sunday when Gwen and Bill went away. I forget where - they didn't go to Gloucester which was his home, they went somewhere else just for a few days.

Anyway, I do remember that Dorothy and I went out for our walk, and I suppose it was the effect of Bill and Gwen's wedding that we got talking about weddings.

---

* The British Legion hall was located at the bottom of the Town Steps, on the north side next to what was then No.5.

## Commitment

Up to that point, as I said, we were still just friends, but I suppose the war years had brought on our feelings a bit more than they had been before. And I know it may not sound very romantic, but we got talking about when we should get engaged. I said I would have to get an engagement ring and I didn't know when my next leave would be, but it might be around my birthday, April 12th. So I told her, 'I'll go back and I'll see whether I can get a ring for you. And I'll let you know when I'm coming home.'

After I was back in camp, I was talking with one of the chaps in our billet there, Geoffrey, and I said, 'Well, I'm hoping to get engaged when I go home next time, and I'm going to go to Leamington Spa and get a ring.' He said, 'Are you wanting a ring?' and I said, 'Yes, I am.' Unfortunately for him, the girl he was going to be engaged to threw the engagement up and gave him the ring back. He said, 'Look, I've got it here,' and I said, 'Well, that's a nice ring.' It was a three-stone twisted band. So I asked him how much he wanted for it. He said he didn't know, he'd forgotten what he paid for it now. I said 'Look, I'll tell you what I'll do. I'll take it, I'll have it valued, I'll get the jeweller give me a statement for the value, and I'll pay whatever he says the value is.'

So that's how I got the engagement ring, and in April, sometime after my birthday, I'd got leave. I did the proper thing and got down on my knee and asked Dorothy to marry me, and put the ring on her finger. It fitted perfectly and she was very pleased with it. And of course, we still have that ring.

*Dorothy's engagement ring*

It was sometime soon after that, that I had a somewhat unexpected visit from Peggy, and that was my opportunity to tell her I was engaged. She had actually come to Leamington Spa and lodged overnight with a couple, Dennis and Zena, which is how I later got to know them. They come back into the story in due course, after the war.

Dorothy and I had decided that if possible, we'd like to get married on July 24th, which was sort of three months ahead. We started fixing up the arrangements for that date - but I still had to confirm whether I could get leave for that date. When we told her mother and father, they said well, that's another wedding we'll need to do. Dorothy's mum said in her quiet way, 'All right, we shall organise everything - we'll see if we can have the reception at the British Legion hut again, let us see to that.' Of course, I said thanks very much indeed. So we started making all the rough arrangements at that stage.

Fortunately, as it turned out, I was able to get leave for that particular week. In fact, on the Thursday before we got married on the Saturday, I was allowed to set off home on the train. However, I did leave the camp a bit late, and when I got to Liverpool Street, I found I could only get as far as Ipswich that night. So at Ipswich station, I asked what time was the first train out in the morning, and they said it was the mail train about half past six, something like that.

Just off the station, just round to the right, there was a canteen. I don't know whether it was run by the YMCA or some other organisation, it wasn't the 'Sally Ann', the Salvation Army. They had a dormitory there with bunks and you could hire a bed for the night. But by the time I got there, all the beds had been taken. 'Sorry, we're full.' Oh dear. So I sat on a tip-up chair (it was one of those folding chairs) leaning up against the wall. That's how I slept on Thursday night - until it was time to go out and catch the train in the morning.

I went straight down to Aldeburgh, I think (I didn't call at Mum's first), unshaven and all the rest of it. I said, 'Well I'm here,' then of course, I went home to Leiston later on the Friday, ready for Saturday.

In the meantime, Mum had organised the taxi for us. Bertie was to be my best man, and his Dorothy was already down on leave at the time (they'd got married the previous September). Mum and Dad, Bertie and Dorothy and me, we were all going down in Mr Lunnis's taxi on the Saturday morning. All the other arrangements had been made by Mum and Dad Chase. Dorothy had already been up to London and got her wedding dress, a white one. I didn't see it until she came into the church. I'd organised someone from Leiston to take photographs, there being no photographer in Aldeburgh at that stage - I got Mr Wardell, who we knew quite well - it was his son actually.

## Wedding and honeymoon (July 1943)

We had our wedding in Aldeburgh Church, had our photographs taken outside, then climbed in the car and were taken round to the Town Steps. The others followed on foot as it wasn't far for them to walk.

As arranged, we had our reception in the British Legion hut by the big steps. And what a spread everyone had done, with those next-door neighbours of Mum and Dad Chase having made a lovely cake - a single tier one for us, but a beautiful cake, iced and everything else.

That night, everyone danced to a wind-up gramophone which was looked after by Randall, Dorothy's little brother. In the end, there was quite a bit of food left over from the reception, so Dorothy and I decided to go outside and invite in some soldiers who had been wandering about. We asked if they'd like to join us, and they did - there were

*The wedding at Aldeburgh Church, 24th July 1943*

89

about six of them I think - they came in and enjoyed the rest of the evening with us.

We had arranged to spend the first night at the house of some friends up on the Saxmundham Road - Mr and Mrs Shipp. They were great friends of Mum and Dad. They'd made their front bedroom all ready for us and so forth. On the Sunday, we went back down to Mum and Dad's, had our breakfast with them, then caught the ten o'clock train from Aldeburgh to London. From there, it was over to Paddington to catch the train to Torquay - because I'd managed to book a hotel at Babbacombe in Devon, for our honeymoon.

I'd been able to book that hotel thanks to the PE instructor at Gaydon, Charles Shepherd, who was a sergeant. He came from down on the south coast quite near there, and he knew the people at the Babbacombe Cliff Hotel. He'd said, 'All right, you write to them, tell them that I've recommended you, and I'm sure they'll be able to fix you up.'

We got down to Torquay nearly on midnight I think it was, and then we had to get a taxi to the hotel in Babbacombe, but the head waiter had stayed up for us. It was closed up when we got there and I had to knock. The head waiter came to the front door and said, 'Oh yes, welcome, and did you know that Italy had capitulated?' I wasn't at all interested, and I said no, I didn't. 'Yes', he said, 'We've heard it on the radio today. And Mussolini is on the run.' Oh, very nice, but we've come to stay. He said, 'Come through, I've got some sandwiches and coffee ready for you.' He took us for a short walk up a path to this house a bit away from the main hotel, and there we had a very nice bedroom actually, with our own bathroom. So that's where we spent our honeymoon.

We had a very pleasant time that week. The only thing with Babbacombe was that you couldn't get down on the beach, as it was all barbed-wired off. They had gun emplacements here, there and everywhere. There had also been a funicular railway, but that was closed down too, so we spent most of the time on top of the cliff during the day. It was beautiful weather - the sun shone the whole week. In fact, I got rather sunburned, as you can imagine.

At the end of our week, we took a taxi back to Torquay to catch the train, which was packed, so we had to sit on our cases in the corridor all the way to Paddington. But we made it there, across London on the Tube to Liverpool Street, then back on the train to Aldeburgh.

## Back to camp (August 1943)

That long trip back was on the Saturday, and I had to return to RAF Gaydon on the Monday. It was straight back into doing air tests with new aircrew trainees.

On 23rd October, I had been on a night flight from Wellesbourne Mountford with one of the pupils, and after I had landed back, my squadron pal Charlie Shepherd had a word with me. He said, 'I'm to tell you you've got to go over to Wellesbourne tomorrow - it looks like you've been posted somewhere.' Well surely not... all right, well I'll see. By the way, there were two Charlie Shepherds, one was the PE instructor and the other one was on the squadron with me, it was he who gave me this message. He came from Ilkley in Yorkshire (as in the song) - and he was a nice chap, was Charles.

Soon the following morning, on the Sunday, I went over to Wellesbourne, checked in, and they said, 'Right, yes, you're being seconded to the Americans.' I said, 'Oh, where?' He said. 'Aldermaston.' I thought, 'Where the Dickens is that?' I didn't know. So of course, I made enquiries, and found out that this Aldermaston was in Berkshire, near Reading.

I enquired what we were going to do there. I was told, 'You and another chap who is going down from Wellesbourne with you, you'll meet up with three others who are coming from other stations. The five of you, one will be a Warrant Officer, the other four are Flight Sergeants.' I said, 'All right.' All he told us at that stage was that we were going to be seconded to the Americans down there.

### RAF Aldermaston (October 1943)

We got there late at night, booked in to the American guardroom, and told them, 'Yes, we've been sent here, just posted here.'

The sergeant said, 'You'd like some food, would you?' I said, 'Well yes, please. You know, we've been travelling all day, we did have something in London, but that was a long time ago.' He said, 'All right,' and he phoned up the cook in the cookhouse. He said to him, 'Look, I've got five limeys here, can you fix some food for them?' The cook must have said, 'Send them up.' So the guard sergeant said, 'Right, I'll take you up.'

He took us up to the cookhouse, saw this cook and he said to us, 'All I can do is some Frankfurters for you.' 'Well, anything at this time of night.' 'Right, Frankfurters it will be.'

He cooked these Frankfurters, served them up on a plate, then he reached up to shelf above him and brought a big tin down - it was cherry jam. He said, 'Now you'll want this with it!' We thought, cherry jam with Frankfurters?

Anyway, we thought, 'Well, we're here, we've got to live like the Americans now.' We had the cherry jam with the Frankfurters and quite enjoyed it. We had some bread with it as well.

And thereafter, of course, we were always eating with the Americans, and came to love it. The Americans were always saying our food is terrible in Britain - but we told them, 'It's lovely here compared with what we'd get in camp.' The one meal I really enjoyed was breakfast: pancakes with maple syrup and crispy bacon. Absolutely lovely, I did used to enjoy that.

Even NCOs* messed in with the ordinary soldiers - they didn't have their own mess. We had been issued with some utensils - there was a metal plate sort of thing, and a mug, a knife, fork and spoon. That took us back to when we were airmen (we'd had those in the RAF), but we quickly got used to it. After our meal, we had to go to a big

---

* non-commissioned officers

tank, clean our own things and keep them with us. But to us, the food was marvellous.

It was an army camp, based at the edge of this airfield, and the American gliders used to come in there on tests or exercises ahead of the planned D-Day landings. They used to fly in and crash[*], and all the rest of it. I suppose they were the equivalent to our Royal Engineers, that type of thing - and they were all very nice chaps, I got to like them very much.

*Library picture of American Waco GC-4 gliders used during D-Day landing*

I think we went down on the Tuesday, and at the end of that first week, the Warrant Officer who was with us told us the liaison officer who was to give us our instructions was based on the other side of the airfield. He would go over that morning and book us in. I said, 'All right, fair enough, you're in charge at the moment.' He said, 'Yes I am, but I shall be going back to camp tomorrow. And, oh yes, as you're the senior flight sergeant, you'll be in charge.' Well thank you very much, I thought.

Off he went, but evidently when he got over there, the officer wasn't in that section, and no one else was. He sort of looked around, and on the desk he saw some blank leave forms, and there was a date stamp beside it. He got the date stamp, got the right date on it, stamped five forms, took them and put them in his pocket, came back to us and said, 'All right, we're going on a weekend leave.' 'Are we?' we said. 'Yes,' he said, 'Fill these in, I've signed them all as the officer, but

---

[*] The single-use gliders were intended for controlled crash-landings for rapid delivery of troops and equipment

93

one of you will have to fill in my one, so the writing doesn't match.'
'Fair enough,' we said.

We then went to the lieutenant - he was in the American forces - and said, 'We've got leave for this weekend.' 'Oh, have you?' 'Yes, Saturday morning we shall be off and we'll be back by midnight on Monday.' 'Sure, OK.' We showed them our passes. So on Saturday morning, off we went after breakfast, hitch-hiking into London.

We were going up the Great West Road in the back of an army truck, when suddenly it stopped. We thought, 'What's up?' and looked out. We saw a cordon across the road, and there was a checkpoint with an officer - I think he was a major, along with a despatch rider and some others. They sort of interrogated the driver of our truck, but they didn't come and look in the back.

As we drove off, of course they saw us in the back. We just laughed and continued. But about two miles up the road, I could see the despatch rider coming up fast behind. I said to the others, 'I've got an idea we're going to be stopped.' The despatch rider did stop us, and said, 'The major has sent me to check on you.' 'Oh yes?' 'Have you got passes?' 'Yes, of course we've got passes.' We said that, thinking thank goodness we had. He said, 'OK, I'll tell the major you're on official weekend leave.' So that was it, and on into London we went.

One of us was going to Norwich, one was going to Birmingham, but I don't know where the other two were going. The Warrant Officer was intending to leave us on the Tuesday. I think I managed to catch the last train, the five past five, which got down to Aldeburgh about eight o'clock at night. Again, I hadn't let Dorothy know in advance as it was all arranged in such a hurry. I couldn't even let Mum and Dad know, so not for the first time, I gave them all a bit of a surprise. Anyway, I had the weekend there, exactly fourteen weeks since we'd got married. We went to the dance that Saturday night, then home to Victoria Road. I think we went to Leiston on the Sunday to see Mum and Dad, then back to Aldeburgh. I left Aldeburgh on the Monday.

Dorothy had to go back to work in the laundry on Monday morning, while I caught the train to London and then returned to

Aldermaston. I booked in, and all was well. It was on the Tuesday that the Warrant Officer said, 'Right, I've now been recalled back to my unit, you're in charge now.' I thought, 'Well, what on earth are we being expected to do here?'

Well, when the instruction finally came, it was that we've got to set up a radio school to teach the English procedures to the wireless operators on the American aircraft that tug the gliders. I said, 'But we've got nothing here, no training manual or anything.' 'Well, you'll have to produce one.' 'We haven't got a classroom.' 'Well, you'll have to get one built.' So we said to the lieutenant, 'Can we have a classroom built?' He said, 'Oh yes, sure, we'll do that.'

He got his men and said, 'Right, these RAF men, they want a classroom built.' They designed a classroom and built it out of all the wooden crates that the gliders had been packed in coming into the country. They built a marvellous classroom. It was big enough for the 25 trainees expected on the course - with blackboards, desks, chairs, and a great big pot-bellied stove in the middle to keep people warm (it was coming up to wintertime). It had everything we needed.

After that, I said to the others, 'Well look, let's divide this up into sections of subjects, I'll do this subject, you'll do that subject, and so forth. Write up your subject so we can get it into a manual.' So they did. I then said, 'Right, can any of you type?' The answer was no. I said, 'Oh well, I can, two fingers, I'll type it up.'

I typed up the manual myself, and then we had the first course come in about a fortnight later, I think. We started teaching these Americans the British wireless procedures, and it actually went quite well.

## Christmas in Suffolk (December 1943)

It was getting towards the end of the year, and the lieutenant said, 'Look, I expect you'd all like to go back on your Christmas holiday with your families, but I can only let one of you go - that's what I've been instructed.' He said, 'I know how we're going to do this - we'll have three long straws and one short straw. The one that draws the short straw will be the one that has the leave.' He got these straws in his hand. I think I took about the third one, and it was the short one!

I said to the others, 'Well look, I'm sorry you didn't get the leave, but I admit I'm very pleased to have it because I can now go home and see my wife.' They said it was all right, they'd expected that three of us would stay here, and told me to go off and enjoy it. And before I went off, the Americans gave me chocolates and all sorts of other things to take home, even some fruit if I remember rightly.

It was the day before Christmas Eve that I went home, and I returned to camp the day after Boxing Day - so I had Christmas at home with Dorothy and both sets of parents, and was able to share out the chocolates between them, and so forth.

In fact, that was the first Christmas that I had at home since I had joined the RAF. The first one, 1940, I'd had at Manston. In 1941, I'd spent Christmas meal in camp: I remember going back to my billet at Woodhall Spa, this old lady's place, and oh dear, going into the local hotel there to find a drink. It was packed with people getting ready for their Christmas, and I'd never felt so lonely in all my life - it was the one time I felt homesick, I must admit. I'd had one drink, then just went to my bed up in the loft. In 1942, I'd spent Christmas at Boston with the Harrisons. But in 1943, I was able to have it at home at Aldeburgh and Leiston. So it worked out quite well in that way.

I returned to camp at Aldermaston, and things carried on as before, training those American pilots. I even managed to get what we called Harwell boxes installed in another building, ready for the second lot of crew members who came in on the course. The Harwell box was a little cabin for a trainee wireless operator, as if they were in an aircraft. There would be perhaps six or eight of these cabins in the class. Outside, in the main part of the building, would be the control room with all the equipment connecting with the boxes. In the cabins, they had to do various exercises on direction-finding.

We got to the end of January, then into February, and then we unexpectedly got a message that we four were all going back to our units. An officer was coming down to take over from us. And so that is what happened - I went back to RAF Gaydon, and this officer took it all over. I left the training manual with him which we had compiled – and it was the one that I had typed myself.

## Back to RAF Gaydon (February 1944)

Back at Gaydon, I thought I'm here until they decide what else they're going to do with me. Then the CO called me in one day and he said, 'We've just had a report about the work you've done with the Americans.' 'Oh yes, sir.' 'They said they've been very pleased with you, it's a good report.' I said, 'Well, we did all work hard on it, and we thought it went all right.' 'Yes,' he said, 'Now, what about taking up a commission?' Well that was the last thing on my mind. An elementary schoolboy, that's what I was really, becoming a commissioned officer in the RAF? That was beyond my wildest dreams. He said, 'Yes, you put it in, and I'll see that it goes forward.'

I got the application form through, put it in with all the details they wanted, education, what other experience I had and all the rest of it. It went forward, and in March I suddenly got a call to go up to RAF Abingdon on an officers' assessment course.

I went to Abingdon, and went through the panel there. Once again, the fact that I'd been with the Americans came up, and they all seemed to like it at that stage. They said, 'Right, we'll recommend you for a commission. It'll be coming through in two or three weeks, and you'll be a Pilot Officer, with a new number. You'll hear more in due course.' I was most chuffed at this.

After I came out of there, I knew I had a couple of days and that I could go home. I went back to Leiston and told my parents that I was going to be an officer. It did rather surprise them – just as it had surprised me. Then I went down to Aldeburgh and saw Dorothy, and told her the news. She seemed pleased about it, but didn't make any other comments really. It was then that she told me, yes, she definitely was pregnant. I told her I'll see if I can get her back to Leamington Spa, near me, if I can.

I returned to Gaydon and set about arranging that - and this is where the people that I'd met when Peggy came down in 1943 come back into the story: Zena and Dennis, and their son Barry. Zena said, 'Yes, you come to Leamington, we'll put Dorothy up here. Of course, you'll have to sleep on a single bed in the big lounge, but there you are.' So I went back home again, picked up Dorothy, and brought her there.

I remember, at that stage, she had only just received her false teeth. I can't remember exactly when she went to the dentist - she had a little bit of a black spot on her top two front teeth, and thought that was the only thing that was wrong. But the dentist said, 'Oh no, I think I better take all your teeth out, then you can have false teeth.' And being Dorothy, she didn't contest it. So she had the bottom ones taken out, then the top ones, and then she had to go back for an impression. It was just before I went to pick her up to bring her to Leamington that she had her false teeth fitted. Very neat they were as well, so when I took her to Leamington, she had a full mouth of teeth.

At the beginning of April, I received notification that my commission had come through. That meant my name would have been printed in the London Gazette. I was now a Pilot Officer, and my new number was 172888.

*Harold in Officer uniform, late 1944*

Going back a bit, the day that I left after the interview at Abingdon in London, I'd gone into the military tailors in Regent Street where I'd heard other people had been*, and they'd fitted me up with all my requisites - two sets of uniform, a great coat, hat and shirts, socks and

---

* This may have been Hector Powe's of 165 Regent Street

so forth. All I had to do was sign a document, then they'd said I could pick it all up as soon as my commission came through.

So when that day came, I said to Dorothy, 'Right, we'll go into London to pick up my uniform, if you'd like to come too.' She said she would like that very much. At the time we went, I'd actually just been promoted to a Warrant Officer, but hadn't even had time to change the stripes on my arm. Anyway, I went into the fitting room as a Flight Sergeant, changed into my officer's uniform, and came out as a Pilot Officer - before everything was then put into a suitcase.

Before we returned to Leamington, we went to a theatre just off Leicester Square and saw a variety show. I can't quite remember the name of the show now, but I do remember we sat up in the circle. It was an afternoon matinee, because we got back to Leamington in the early evening.

When I reported back the following day to Gaydon, the first thing they said was, 'Oh, now you've been made an officer, you're going back to Wellesbourne Mountford.' It wasn't far away, so I could still get into Leamington quite easily.

## Return postings (April 1944)

Back at Wellesbourne Mountford, I was posted in the student section there. It was the same place where four or five of us had previously done some of our training when we went through our OTU. The chap in charge was a Flight Lieutenant Finch, quite nice, and he was billeted out in a big house in Stratford with his wife. A lot of the officers were also there - they'd taken over this big mansion.

Later that year, I was one of four to be invited (a formal invitation, I might add) to a sort of a party at this mansion, together with the wives of the officers and so forth. The four of us went and we had quite a nice evening, with games and a treasure hunt through the grounds, and some nice food and drink, of course. Then when it was over, a truck picked us all up and took us back to camp. That was the first time I

*Official photograph labelled No.14 course ACOS, the Air Crew Officers School at Hereford, in 1944. Harold is third from left, middle standing row.*

learned how to reply to an official invitation. To start with, we had all been at a loss as to how to do this, but Finch said all you do is… this and that. So a little bit more of my education was added to me then.

During this time, I'd been Orderly Officer a couple of times, I'd also been Signals Officer a couple of times, which meant me staying on duty overnight. I didn't particularly like that aspect, but it was OK.

Then in September 1944, I was posted to RAF Hereford (it was just outside Hereford actually) on an aircrew officers' school. This was where we learned more about the etiquette of being an officer, such as on parade and that sort of thing. We also had an assault course to go through, along with the marching and all that sort of stuff, and the school went on for three weeks. Then soon after I was back at Wellesbourne, I was told I was being posted back to Gaydon - which pleased me, as I liked Gaydon very much.

## Fatherhood (July 1944)

D-Day came on June 6th, but about three weeks before that, Dorothy had said to me, 'I'm getting near time, and I'd like to go back to Aldeburgh to have the baby.' I don't think D-Day had actually taken place then, but London was being attacked, suffering these V-bombs, the first ones. I managed to negotiate through central London with my heavily pregnant wife, and got her back to Aldeburgh, which was the place she had said she wanted to set herself up to have the baby. When it came to the event, it turned out to be a nursing home out at Eye, quite a long way away from Aldeburgh.

Back at Wellesbourne, I'd already told the CO that Dorothy was expecting a baby, and that I might get a telegram any day. He'd said, 'All right, when you get it, just give me a shout, off you go and don't worry about anything.' I said thanks very much.

On July 20th, I received a telegram from Mum Chase to say that a baby boy had been born at Eye. I'd been on duty the previous night, I would have been either duty Signals Officer or Orderly Officer, so I was still asleep in bed when the batswoman came in. She said, 'Oh sir, there's a telegram waiting for you down in the office,' so I guessed what it was straight away.

I quickly grabbed my little bit of kit that I wanted to take with me, and went in and saw the CO. He said, 'Righty-ho, see you when you come back.' I didn't tell him I'd be back at a particular time, but I knew it would be in five days or something like that. I hitch-hiked to London (there was no other way of getting there quickly), and caught a late train getting into Ipswich, arriving sometime after nine. I thought, somehow I've got to get myself up to Eye. I walked outside the station and there was a taxi there, so I said to the driver, 'Can you take me to Eye Maternity Home?' He said, 'Sorry, it's outside my area.' I said, 'Oh dear, my wife's just given birth to a baby - and I've got a telegram to say it was born yesterday...' He said, 'You've got a telegram with you? That'll do, as long as you've got that, if we get stopped, I've got cover.' So off we went, he drove me to the nursing home at Eye, and I got there a bit after 10 o'clock.

I saw the night sister and announced who I was, and she said, 'Oh yes, I'll take you up to see Dorothy in a minute. Have you booked in anywhere?' I told her no. She said, 'Ah, I see... now can you ride a bicycle?' I said, 'Oh, yes.' 'Right, while you see your wife, I'll see if I can organise something... I have my bicycle here and if I can find another one, we can ride out to my home. In the meantime, I'll telephone my husband to warn him that you're coming.' I thought, that's very kind, thinking her home would be on the outskirts of Eye.

I went up, they drew the curtains round Dorothy's bed, and I think Tony was in the cot beside her, so I saw him. Dorothy was surprised and pleased to see me, of course. I told her the night sister was getting me home to her place to stay, and finding a bicycle for me, to be able to get there and back. The night sister asked me how long I was staying. I said I thought I could stay until Monday: this was Thursday, and Tony was born on the Wednesday. She said, 'All right, you can come in to see your wife in the morning, afternoon and evening while you're here, and you can make use of the bicycle.' I thanked her very much. I was thinking that maybe I might walk it instead.

After seeing Dorothy, I went off with the night sister on our bikes, and we cycled... and we cycled... and we cycled... right out in the countryside. I was thinking, 'Where the devil does she live?' She said, 'It's quite easy, keep straight on along this road and you'll come back into Eye.' We finally arrived at a big house on a corner. She knocked on the door, her husband came, she introduced me, and then she said, 'Look, I'm going back to duty now, so I'll leave you with my husband, he'll make you something to eat and drink.' I hadn't had much at all, so I was thankful for that.

I forget what he made - some toast and scrambled egg, something like that. It turned out that he was an amateur, but very enthusiastic, photographer. He'd got masses of photographs he wanted to show me. His wife had acted as a model for him, and in a semi-nude state too! He was very proud of his photos, and they were actually quite good. However, it was about four in the morning before I got to bed.

He'd told me that when his wife came in off duty, he expected that she would bring me a cup of tea. I was quick going off to sleep and that was it, but I woke next morning, in daylight, and I could hear voices outside the window. I thought, what's going on? I looked out and there was a group of youths, lots of them. Just then, there was a knock on the door and in came the night sister with a cup of tea, so I asked her, 'Is this a school?' She said, 'Yes, it is a sort of a school, actually, it's a borstal. They're all delinquents - and my husband is a housemaster in there.'

I got up and had a shower, shaved (I had my shaving gear with me), dressed and went down to a very nice breakfast with the nurse - her husband had by then gone on duty. She said, 'Are you going off to see your wife?' I said, 'Yes.' She said, 'Don't forget, go straight along this road...' So that is what I did - and again in the afternoon and once more in the evening. I think I found a little place where I could get some food at midday, but when I got back to the house, he had a meal prepared for me anyway. This went on Friday, Saturday and Sunday, then on Monday I knew I had to go back to camp,

That day, having seen Dorothy in the morning, I phoned up for a taxi to take me to the nearest station, and left the bicycle along with many thanks to the owner, whoever that was. I'd said my goodbyes to the night nurse when I left the house that morning, and the taxi took me to Diss railway station, from where I travelled back via London to Leamington Spa.

I went in and saw the CO, and told him, 'Look, Dorothy's had a baby boy.' He wished me well, and said he hoped to see them soon. I told him I'd see what I could arrange to pick them up. In the event, I was able to do that when Tony was three weeks old. I got them back to Leamington Spa, and she stayed there until after D-Day.

I was still at Gaydon, and I had been Signals Officer all the time, a job that I got to enjoy. I also played hockey for the station, thanks to Sergeant Shepherd, the PE instructor - he was one of the people I'd previously met when I was a Flight Sergeant there. Chas was the one who'd originally put me in touch with Babbacombe Cliff Hotel. After he'd asked me whether I played hockey, and I'd said, 'No, never,' he said, 'Well let me give you instruction,' and promptly put me in the team. It was a mixed team, with WAAFs playing alongside airmen. I was put at centre-forward, and we went all over the place playing hockey for the camp.

That went on until it came to VE Day in May, which we celebrated in Leamington. We went out that night and it was certainly a lively evening in the town.   And then the day after VE Day, I was told that I was going to be posted to Abingdon, which was 10 Group Headquarters.   So I said, 'Right, I've got to take Dorothy and Tony back to Suffolk now,' which I did.   That would be in about June 1945.

I returned to Gaydon, then went off to Abingdon as instructed.   I was only there a little while, and they then sent me on a course to RAF Finningley.

*Harold, Dorothy and Tony in 1945*

## RAF Finningley (June 1945)

It wasn't an officer's school as such, but it was something similar.[*] We were all officers, and the school was teaching us all about signals, radar and so forth, but with civilian psychologists who were doing assessments on us as well.

We all had to do an opening talk of ten minutes on any subject we liked, and I spoke about my experience with the Americans.   A chap

---

[*] It was BCIS Finningley, Bomber Command Instructors School

was marking me while I was giving this talk. I went through the course and I think I was up there for a fortnight. Anyway, I got an 'A2' pass. There had only ever been three or four A1s, and there were just two or three of us got A2s on this course, so I thought, that's quite good.

Following that course, I once again went back to Gaydon, but hadn't been there long before VJ Day came along. The next day after that, I was posted back to Finningley to the Signals Instructors Unit - this time on the staff. And I don't mind admitting, I went on to thoroughly enjoy my time there. I found myself teaching others what I had once learned at the same place. And that went on right until the time I was demobbed.

The Squadron Leader who was in charge of the section was a good musician and pianist - he used to write songs - and so he took charge of the camp concert party. He wanted a stage manager. We all had nicknames and my name was Charlie. One day, he said to me, 'Charlie, you're my stage manager.' I asked what that meant, and what I should do. He told me to see to the lights, the curtains, all the sound effects and all the rest of it. 'All right,' I said, 'I'll see to it.'

So I became part of the camp concert party, and we went all over Yorkshire, to miners' clubs and other places with this group. We were out quite often two or three times a week. The only trouble was, because we were late out and got back late, the bar would normally be closed in the officers' mess.

Our camp commandant, the Group Captain, looked exactly like Edward G Robinson and was a bit of a lad. He would sometimes keep the bar in the mess open until the early hours of the morning. So when The Boss was there, we'd creep in and wonder if the CO was around, and whether we'd be caught. One night, he was there and saw us - we got dragged out to the bar and had to stay there until about 4 o'clock in the morning, having one or two drinks with him.

## A visit to Berlin (December 1945)

*Towards the end of his RAF career, in mid-December 1945, Harold was posted on a trip which formed part of what was called Operation Spasm. This was being run by Bomber Command as a sort of sight-seeing tour to war-torn Germany, mainly for the benefit of ground staff, many of whom would not hitherto have experienced flying. These trips started in Summer 1945 and were known as 'Cooks Tours'.*

*Harold was part of the crew which flew in a Lancaster (number HK761) from Finningley to Berlin on 14th December. The plane landed at Tibenham in south Norfolk on the way, presumably to pick up passengers. They flew into what by then was known as RAF Gatow on the south-west side of Berlin, an airfield that had been captured by the Red Army then handed over to the British. They returned via Tibenham the following day.*

*Harold only shared detailed recollections about this visit much later when, at the age of 91, he was taken on a trip to Berlin to visit his grandson who was living there, the first time he had returned in nearly 67 years. That original visit had made a strong impression on him, seeing a hungry population still living in the largely destroyed city, and the stark division between the Soviet and Western zones.*

*He told of seeing groups of women engaged in clear-up work, a rampant black-market in cigarettes, watches, silk stockings and perfume sold out of briefcases, and people even offering to sell military vehicles in exchange for luxury goods. He remembered the heavy Russian military presence guarding the Brandenburg Gate, with guns pointing at the Western visitors,*

Harold's pass to the Officer's Club in Berlin

106

and the exclusive officer club based in a grand building in Brahmsstrasse in Grunewald, for which he had been given his own membership card.

And as other 'tourists' must have done given the opportunity, he jogged a lap around the track at the Olympic Stadium where Jesse Owens had famously run in front of Hitler in 1936. What thoughts must have been going through his head as he stood there leaning on his stick in silence in 2012, looking at the same empty stadium?[*]

*Pariser Platz and the Brandenburg Gate in May 1945*

---

[*] See photograph on the rear cover of this book

**Demobilisation** (March 1946)

After a time, I had been made up to the rank of Flight Lieutenant because I'd remained a Flying Officer for six months. That came through the very day before I was demobbed from the RAF.

The CO, the chap who looked like Edward G Robinson, called me in, because it wasn't everyone who was going to be demobbed, and he said, 'Right, how would you feel about staying in instead?' I said, 'I'd like to, sir, but I'm married now, and it's a bit hard for my family. I think that I'd like to go back into civilian life.'

He asked what I had done before I joined up, and I said I was a cost clerk, and was hoping to eventually qualify as a cost accountant. 'Oh,' he said, 'How about becoming a teacher, bearing in mind your results on the course?' 'No, I think I'll go back to my civilian job if you don't mind.' He said, 'well, *I* don't mind, but I'm just putting the options to you.' He said, 'If you find after a while that you would rather be back in the RAF, come back. Of course, you'd have to go back to Flying Officer to start with, but there you are.'

So anyway, that's how I was demobbed.

There was a Squadron Leader bomb aimer who was on the staff there. He was going to be demobbed at the same time as me, and he had a car. He drove us both down to Uxbridge, to the very same place where I had signed up more than six years previously. We were duly demobbed, and the following day we went to Wembley Stadium where all the civilian clothes were being issued, the suits and trilbies and what have you.

Then I took the train home. We got to Ipswich, and Dad and one of his workmates happened to be waiting for a train on their way home for the weekend. There they were, and I just said, 'Hello.' There was me. So I made it home.

You might think it would have felt strange being demobbed from the RAF after all that had happened. Well, I didn't know what to feel.

## PART V: Settling to civilian life

### A house and a home (June 1946)

After a week's demobbing leave, I said to Dorothy, 'Let's go and have a bit of a holiday at Leamington Spa.' I'd put my name down at the council for a house at Leiston, but I didn't think we would get one. Before we went off to Leamington, Mum had found out about a house that was going to be empty - it was at number 86 Haylings Road, and it was owned by Mr Powell, who used to run the White Horse Hotel where Connie worked all those years ago. I knew Mr Powell and he knew me. She said, 'You should go and see him, and see if there's any chance of you having that house.'

It was while we were at Leamington Spa, having this bit of a holiday in April 1946, that I got a telegram from Mum to say 'You've got the house at Haylings Road, but you'll have to come and see it.' So I left Dorothy there with Tony, got back to Leiston about eight o'clock, at night and walked in on Mum. She said, 'First you must have some food, then you go and look at the house.' I did, and went off just as it was starting to get dark.

Mr Powell owned a terrace row of six houses, then he had got his house built onto the end of that. When I went and saw him, he said, 'Oh, come in Harold, yes, I didn't really recognise you, because you were always in uniform before.' I said, 'Well, it's about the house, Mr Powell.' He said the council were a bit concerned about offering it to just anyone, because he (the owner) was living on the end. You see, tenancy was still regulated by the government in law, and the council had the say who could have it and who couldn't. 'Would you like to go and see it?' I said, 'Yes, please.' He said, 'Well here's the key, but I'll warn you, that house has been fumigated.' This was evidently because a Mr Barnard (I think his name was) had lived there on his own for over 20 years, and really hadn't done a single thing to the inside. 'Anyway,' he said, 'you can go in, the electricity is on.'

I went there and opened the front door. The dust on the floor was nearly ankle-deep. I walked into the living room, and there was an empty milk bottle on the hearth - and it was green. Around the mantlepiece, he'd got one of those green things with brass studs in, I forget what they used to call them, but it shows how old it was. I thought, 'Oh, I can't bring Dorothy back here.' Anyway, I put the light out and went back to Mum, but kept hold of the key. I told her about it, and she said, 'Look, wait until the morning. I'll bring my brushes and cleaning things, and we'll see what we can do to make it a bit more respectable, before you make a final decision.'

After breakfast the next day, I went off to the house with Mum, and all her brooms and other tackle. We went in, and I said, 'Just look at that!' but she told me not to worry, and we got cracking on it. By the time the day had finished, the place looked different – well, at least it had been cleaned up a bit.

I thought, that's all right, but I've got to get it redecorated, because that's what really would help. So next day, off to the council I went, and saw the clerk Mr Wardell, who once again I knew – although he didn't know me very well, as it was his brother I knew better, the photographer at our wedding. I said, 'Yes, I'd like to have the house, but I feel that it could do with redecorating from top to bottom, I mean inside.' He said it would be a hard job to get all the materials and find people to do the work. I said, 'Well, could I just have permission to get the materials first of all?' 'All right,' he said, 'as you've got a child and you've been in the RAF all that time, I think we're able to award you the house.' And he gave me a slip to authorise buying the decorating materials, sandpaper and sugar soap and that sort of thing, including distemper, which was the wall paint we had in those days.

In the end, it took me twelve weeks, working mostly at night (I was back at my job at the works during the day), and Mum also used to go up during the day. My brother Bertie and Dorothy helped a bit - they were around for a time, because Bertie was back working at Ives shop

- but Dorothy was itching to get back to Leeds. We had to scrape a mass of paper off the walls, not just one layer – but four or five. The middle bedroom had been papered but then distempered bright red, so working on that, it looked like a slaughterhouse, you can imagine!

Anyway, we got all the paper off, and I managed to get someone we knew to do the decorating in the evenings and at weekends - I can't remember his name, they lived down Eastward Ho (his son got killed in a bombing raid on Leiston). Top to bottom, everything was painted cream – that's because it

*86 Haylings Road, Leiston in 2020 – it is located almost opposite the former Volunteer PH*

was the only colour we could get. There were some doors which were left dark brown - we just washed them down to get them clean.

At last, we could move in. I then had to buy utility furniture, but we couldn't get curtains, because we hadn't got coupons at that stage. We just had to make do and mend for everything. Funnily enough, I've still got the dressing table - but that's the only thing I have got left out of that lot. We managed to get a little settee and a couple of easy chairs for the front room, a square of lino on the floor, both in the front room and in the living room, which was where the stairs went up.

The house had three bedrooms. One was a little back room which was sort of over the stairs - it was quite a nice room with a window overlooking the garden.

I think it was the end of July or beginning of August of 1946 that we moved in. In the meantime, out of my demob money, I had bought Dorothy a bicycle and a child's seat to go on the back of it, so she could transport Tony around. At weekends, I used to take him out on it, while Dorothy got the Sunday lunch ready.

Outside the back door was an earth pathway, which was a bit messy, but I was able to get a chap to come and concrete that. We had an outside lavatory, and a coal shed - it was of course all coal fires in the place. At the end of the garden, there was a passageway at the back of the six houses that led back round to Haylings Road, then a very long garden which was overrun by blackberry bushes - it hadn't been tended for years. Not being a gardener myself in any shape or form, I got a chap with a flamethrower to come and burn it all down, and even then, I only cultivated a small portion - I never got round to doing anything else.

So we got everything a little more respectable, but there wasn't much left of my demob money by the time we'd finished. I'd spent the bulk of my RAF money on the redecoration of the house.

We lived there quite happily for a time. I had my bicycle, so we were able to go out picnicking together like we used to, and of course we often went down to Aldeburgh to see Dorothy's folks.

Then in 1947, Zena and Dennis, who had kept in contact with me, wrote again. Two or three times, Zena had said in a letter, 'Why don't you come back to Leamington to work?' and I'd said to Dorothy, 'Oh no... no chance of that.' By then, I was getting on in the cost office at the works - they had made me up into a bit more than a clerk, and I was directly under Mr Tonge, the cost accountant. However, Dennis and Zena had been very good to us when we lived there, so I said to Dorothy, 'Should we invite Dennis and Zena and Barry here for a holiday?' 'Yes,' she said, 'that would be nice.' So I wrote to them, and they chose a fortnight in August. That was when I was able to have a holiday from the cost office.

They came down on the train, and I met them at Leiston station. Of course, they had to walk to ours from the station - which was a bit of a job for Zena getting up Gas Hill. They settled in to our place, and I was able to take them on a tour of Thorpeness and Aldeburgh as well as visit Mum and so forth - so they had quite a nice holiday.

**Coventry calls** (September 1947)

They'd only been back a fortnight when I got another letter from Zena enclosing an advert for a job for a building firm at Coventry - with a house going with it. So I said to Dorothy, 'What do you think I should I do?' She said, 'Well, if you think you really could do that job...' I said, 'I'll try, I may not get it anyway...'

So I wrote an application to this firm, E.K.Youell & Son Limited. A fortnight later, I got a letter back asking if I could come on an interview. It was going to be on a Saturday. I said to Dorothy, 'I'll have to travel up to Leamington on the Friday, to get to Coventry on the Saturday morning.'

I did what I used to do in wartime - I caught the midnight train from Paddington down to Leamington Spa, thinking I would be able to stop overnight with Zena and Dennis. But when I got there, they had gone away for the weekend, or so I learnt from the people in the flat in their basement. So I went into the town, and booked into a hotel there that I knew of, for bed and breakfast. The next morning, I got myself ready and caught the bus to Coventry.

I'd only been to Coventry once before, that was during 1943, when I was hitch-hiking on the way to Leicester, so I didn't really know my way around. I saw a bus supervisor, told him I wanted to get to the Leicester Road, and he told me I needed the No.6 up the Walsgrave Road. The bus turned the corner by the cinema, went up the hill and I got off at Mellowdew Road.

I looked around and could see the place where I had to go for the interview. Now, this is the honest truth, as I stood there, sort of getting my bearings, something said to me, 'You're going to get that job - and you're going to live in that house right there.' I thought, 'Oh...'

There were six of us in the interview, and I got the job. And of course, that meant I got the house that came with it - and it was precisely the one I thought it was - a lovely big house, with a garden. It was one of four belonging to the firm, and quite close to the office - perhaps a little too close to the office in the end.

I told them I would have to give in my notice at the Leiston Works, and would be able to start on the 1st October, something like that. So off I went back home, and told Dorothy that I've got the job. I'd got the house, I'll need to give my notice in, and we'll have to arrange to move.

Smythe's of Leiston were the only removal people we had in the town then, and so I arranged for them to come and empty the house at Haylings Road. It was organised for Dorothy and Tony to travel in their lorry up to Coventry, and then we'd go on to Leamington Spa. We were going to stay there with Zena while we got sorted out at Coventry. I went up a week beforehand, living with Zena and travelling to Coventry every day.

My office was outside the main office building, in the yard, and I shared it with another cost clerk. Through a hatchway window were two surveyors. There was a woodwork unit in the grounds, and another office up there with an elderly man who did all the wages. Youell's were doing quite a big building job at Coventry Hospital, and they had just been awarded another contract for a new hotel at Baginton Airport. The firm owned a terrific amount of property, and had quite a large workforce as well.

I got myself established there, and found they had a very antiquated costing system. I thought, well, I would put my experience from Leiston into operation and see how it goes. So I did, and I used to sit at home doing lists in the evenings. After a while, I was able to put forward some of my ideas to the Company Secretary, Mr Thomson.

I got on well with Mr Thomson. Funnily enough, he lived down Mellowdew Road, just where I got off the bus. His wife took Dorothy to the cinema, and he took me to the theatre once, to see *Carmen*.

One idea I put to him was to have everything put onto punch card - they had that sort of equipment at Leiston when I returned after the war. Each job would have a card, and I set up a coding system, altering their system so as to have everything in view. I was eventually given a room of my own in the main office upstairs, and I used to produce three sheets of charts every month, and it worked all right.

One day the young Mr Youell, who was running the business as his father was partly retired, must have said to Mr Thomson, 'Get our accountant to come and check over what young Rouse was doing,' (or something like that), and this accountant came along to me. He said, 'Well, it's quite good, but it must be a lot of work for you.' I said, 'Well yes, it is, but I think that this is giving us a chance to find out, on a monthly basis, exactly how things are going.' He said, 'Yes, I quite agree, especially if you were able to integrate it into the financial accounts as well...', and so it went on like that.

*The Rouse family in 1950*

The new hotel was coming to completion towards the end of 1950. And the day it was opened, early in 1951, we were all invited over there. I remember that well, because it was the day that I decided to give up smoking.

It had started to become a hard job getting hold of cigarettes, and Dorothy tried getting them in the town for me - but the price kept going up too. I thought, no, and decided to give up. And I kept to it.

Anyway, off we went to Baginton to the opening of this hotel. And people kept saying to me, 'Have a cigarette.' 'No thank you.' 'Go on, have a cigarette!' 'No thank you, I've given up.'

I think Dorothy must have suffered for the first six months, but I stuck to it, and I haven't smoked since.

## To Norwich

*It was soon after that, in 1951, that Dorothy reminded Harold of their longstanding aspiration to settle in Norwich. Coventry was a long way from where she had grown up, and she said she wanted to live nearer the sea.*

*Harold got in touch with his sister Connie, and asked her to keep a look-out for suitable job advertisements. A while later, she forwarded a cutting for a cost clerk at a building firm in Norwich - which turned out to be John Youngs Builders on City Road. He travelled back for an interview and was offered the job. There was no house with the job this time, but Connie offered to put the three of them up in her Thorpe St Andrew bungalow (Margetson Avenue) while they found somewhere to live, having put their furniture into store.*

*They left Coventry in May 1951, and after a time were able to take out a mortgage on a small semi-detached bungalow in nearby South Hill Road, thanks to a loan from Harold's brother Ernie which enabled them to pay the initial deposit. Tony went to school at Hillside Avenue School, and Dorothy took a job with Purdy's Bakers in central Norwich. Later on, Tony moved to the new St William's Way School, and Dorothy changed her job after she found the constant handling of flour gave her dermatitis.*

*In 1952, Harold began home study for the Institute of Cost & Works Accountants professional qualifications, and he passed the intermediate exam in 1953. He was in a position to advance his career, and soon found a*

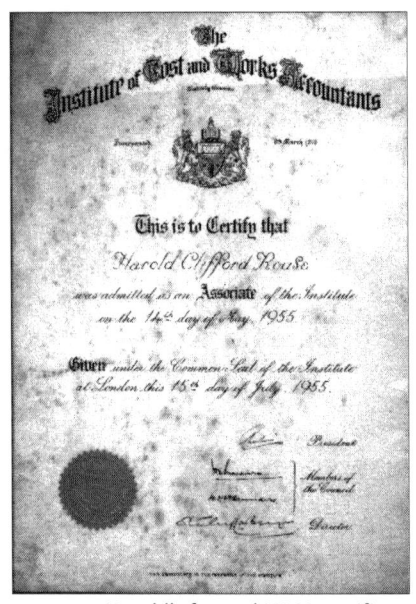

*Harold's framed ICMA certificate*

*new job as accountant for Delecta Table Waters in King Street, part of Morgan's Brewery. Two years later, after much hard work studying in the evenings, he had passed his final examinations and was promoted to Company Secretary – but only after his predecessor had been unceremoniously removed by the chairman Sir Robert Bignold (his customary approach to managing his staff). Not wanting to go the same way in due course, Harold sought a new position. He joined Anglia Building Products, who were able to provide a lift for him daily to their concrete factory in Lenwade, to the west of Norwich.*

*Although it was a generally happy time living at South Hill Road, in winter 1955, the family were involved with an unfortunate incident that occurred in the attached bungalow, whereby a neighbour committed suicide by gassing herself. Harold had found her and was required to appear as a witness at the subsequent inquest.*

*In 1957, Dorothy found she was expecting again, and their daughter Amanda was born in the Spring. At the same time, Harold moved on to a less dusty working environment at car firm Mann Egerton, based at Cromer Road, but he soon discovered that the vital accounts were being run from their central office in Prince of Wales Road. Months later, he moved again to a small engineering company based not far away, at Salhouse Road. That employment lasted until 1959, when the firm ran into financial difficulties and receivers were called in. Harold worked alongside them to rescue the firm.*

*In the meantime, Anglian Building Products had expanded, and an opportunity arose for Harold to return there as Company Secretary, housed in a proper office this time. It was soon afterwards that he was able to buy his first car, a red Mini, and in it he drove daily to Lenwade, usually picking up another employee on the way.*

*In 1961, the family of four made the short move to a more spacious house at St Catherine's Road, Norwich. Unfortunately, the stairs did not suit Dorothy's asthma, so in 1963, they relocated to a new bungalow, at Green Lane West in the nearby village of Rackheath. Four years after that, they moved back to the outskirts of Norwich into a larger bungalow, at Thunder Lane, Thorpe St Andrew.*

By 1968, Anglia Building Products were being taken over by Readymix Concrete, leading to reorganisation and local staff redundancies. Harold was well-placed to depart by choice, and stepped into the vacant post of Company Secretary at the holiday firm Blakes, who were moving their office from London up to Wroxham in the Norfolk Broads.

Harold and the Managing Director of Blakes, in 1984

He had also become increasingly involved in the local branch of his professional body, the Institute of Cost & Management Accountants, having served as Branch President, and organising their annual exams at Norwich's Assembly House. His time at Blakes saw successful expansion of that business, with Harold being responsible for the introduction of new accounting and cost management systems. There he remained to the completion of his career.

With Dorothy at their diamond wedding anniversary, in 2003

A long retirement followed, latterly caring for Dorothy, who spent her last two years in a residential home and who predeceased him in 2008.

In 2012, at the age of 91, Harold joined his family on a trip to see his grandson in Berlin, a city he had last visited 67 years previously.

At the Brandenburg Gate with granddaughter, in November 2012

In 2013, he was belatedly sent his official war medals recognising his war service[*], and he died peacefully in 2014.

---

[*] The 1939-45 Star, Air Crew Europe Star, Defence Medal, and War Medal 1939-45

# EPILOGUE

Harold Rouse's service in the Royal Air Force occupied just six years at the very start of a long adult life. He then embarked on a new career, which to the outside observer followed a reasonably conventional course - albeit one in which he achieved considerable professional status in the end, given his humble family upbringing. Nevertheless, the times he went through as a wartime wireless operator and air gunner must have been deeply formative in his outlook on life in all that followed.

Harold entered his RAF service rather earlier than some of the other veterans who have set down their Bomber Command experiences. Indeed, he was something of a pioneer in respect of the frontline deployment of the legendary Lancaster bomber. His log book has survived[*] as a valuable record containing detailed information about all of his wartime flying while he was on duty. From that log, it is possible to extract precise statistical facts - an idea that would hopefully have appealed to his accounting instincts.

Aircrew were required to maintain, among other things, a running total of the hours spent in the air, as clocked up on a variety of aircraft types. In Harold's case, these are carefully listed as the Dominie, Proctor, Blenheim, Anson, Wellington, Manchester and of course the Lancaster.

At the bottom of the final page of his log book, his total flying hours by day is recorded as 193.2, and that by night 264.3 hours. Added together, this equates to a total of more than 19 days spent continuously in the air. Much of that was in aircraft which had less-than-perfect reputations for safety or reliability, even when flown in

---

[*] A digital copy has been made available to the International Bomber Command Centre in Lincoln (www.internationalbcc.co.uk)

benign conditions. In the course of being trained, and also when later training others, he must have experienced hundreds of take-offs and landings. These included what were known for good reason as 'circuits and bumps' with inexperienced pilots at the controls. It is a wonder that his record includes so few physical mishaps.

Over the course of his tour of active duty with 97 Squadron (concentrated entirely into 1942), Harold went out on 28 recorded combat operations over hostile territory. They accounted for a total of 173.4 hours of flying in unfriendly conditions, almost entirely at night. His experience on these flights must have amounted to an unhealthy cocktail of boredom, fatigue and occasional extreme fear.

It is worth considering this level of exposure in the context of the total of recorded Bomber Command casualties, whereby 46 per cent of the 125,000 aircrew were killed outright in service, and a further 15 per cent were either wounded or became prisoners of war.[*]

Of course, there was much more to life as RAF aircrew than the time spent flying operationally, and it is hoped that Harold's verbal account transcribed here gives an accurate impression of the sort of things that went on in camp and while on leave.

From his own close shaves (recorded or otherwise) and especially through the loss of his friends, Harold surely realised for himself how fortunate he was to have survived his tour of duty. That awareness must have been ever-present for the remainder of his time in the RAF, and then continued in the background throughout the many civilian years that followed.

After his long life, Harold's ashes lie buried in Aldeburgh Churchyard, alongside those of his beloved wife Dorothy.

---

[*] Calculated from accurate figures given by W.R. Chorley (author of *RAF Bomber Command Losses: Roll of Honour* (2007), as quoted on the Wikipedia website

# PICTURE SOURCES AND CREDITS

The editor and publisher have made every effort to ensure that the necessary permissions have been obtained for illustrations used in this book.

Grateful thanks are due to those who have agreed to allow material to be shared. If any oversights are brought to our attention, these will of course be rectified in any future edition.

Most pictures have been sourced from the Rouse family collection, but the following images were obtained from external sources:

Page 80, Lancaster R5609, picture courtesy Wally's War blog, https://wallyswar.wordpress.com

Page 82, junction of Horncastle Road and Hospital Lane, Boston, semi-panoramic view in May 2019, courtesy Google Streetview

Page 93, D-day gliders, historical library picture, courtesy www.fiddlersgreen.net/models

Page 107, Pariser Platz and Brandenburg Gate, Berlin in 1945, courtesy Wikipedia, creative commons, attribution tormentor4555

Rear cover, Lancaster image top right, courtesy John Beavin, BBMF at Coningsby 1979, www.dpreview.com/forums

# APPENDIX 1

## Harold Rouse in the family tree

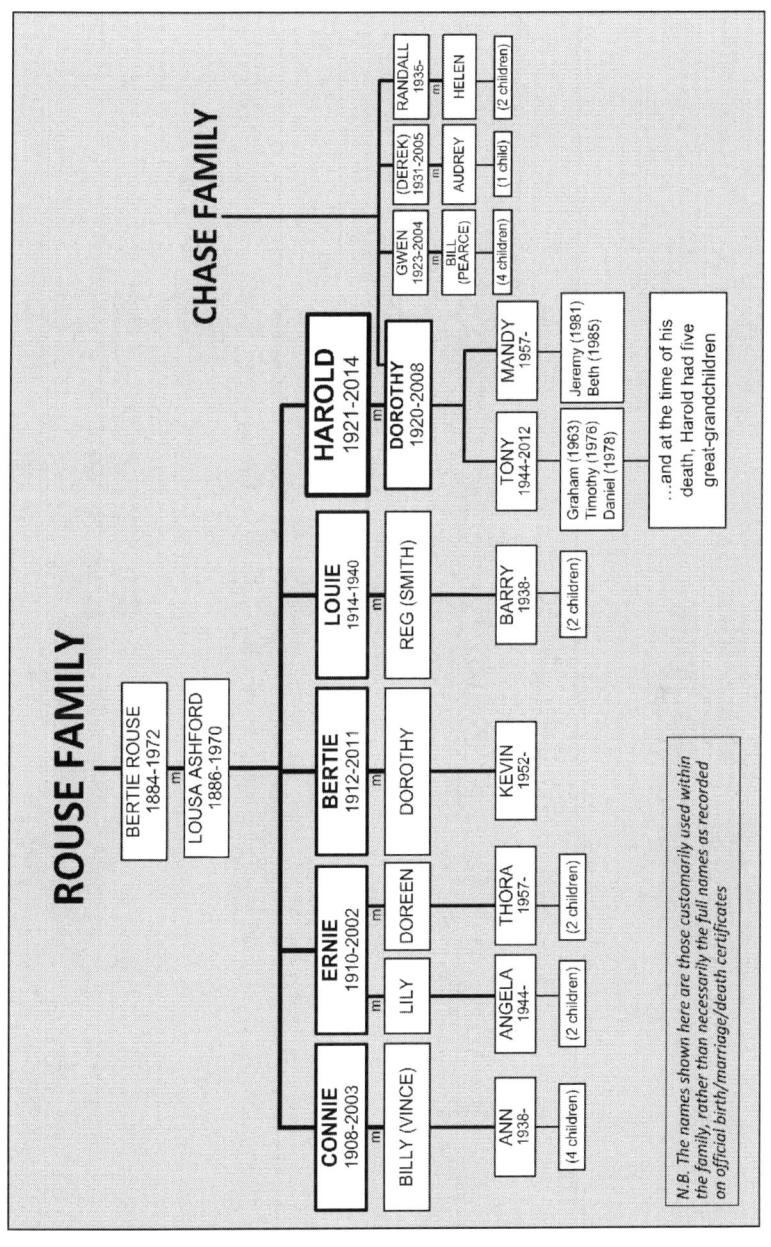

**ROUSE FAMILY**

**CHASE FAMILY**

BERTIE ROUSE 1884-1972
m
LOUSA ASHFORD 1886-1970

HAROLD 1921-2014
m
DOROTHY 1920-2008

CONNIE 1908-2003
m
BILLY (VINCE)

ERNIE 1910-2002
m
LILY

BERTIE 1912-2011
m
DOROTHY

LOUIE 1914-1940
m
REG (SMITH)

GWEN 1923-2004
m
BILL (PEARCE)

(DEREK) 1931-2005
m
AUDREY

RANDALL 1935-
m
HELEN

ANN 1938-
(4 children)

ANGELA 1944-
(2 children)

THORA 1957-
(2 children)

DOREEN

KEVIN 1952-

BARRY 1938-
(2 children)

TONY 1944-2012
Graham (1963)
Timothy (1976)
Daniel (1978)

MANDY 1957-
Jeremy (1981)
Beth (1985)

(4 children)

(1 child)

(2 children)

...and at the time of his death, Harold had five great-grandchildren

*N.B. The names shown here are those customarily used within the family, rather than necessarily the full names as recorded on official birth/marriage/death certificates*

# APPENDIX 2

## Sketch-map showing the area around Leiston, Suffolk

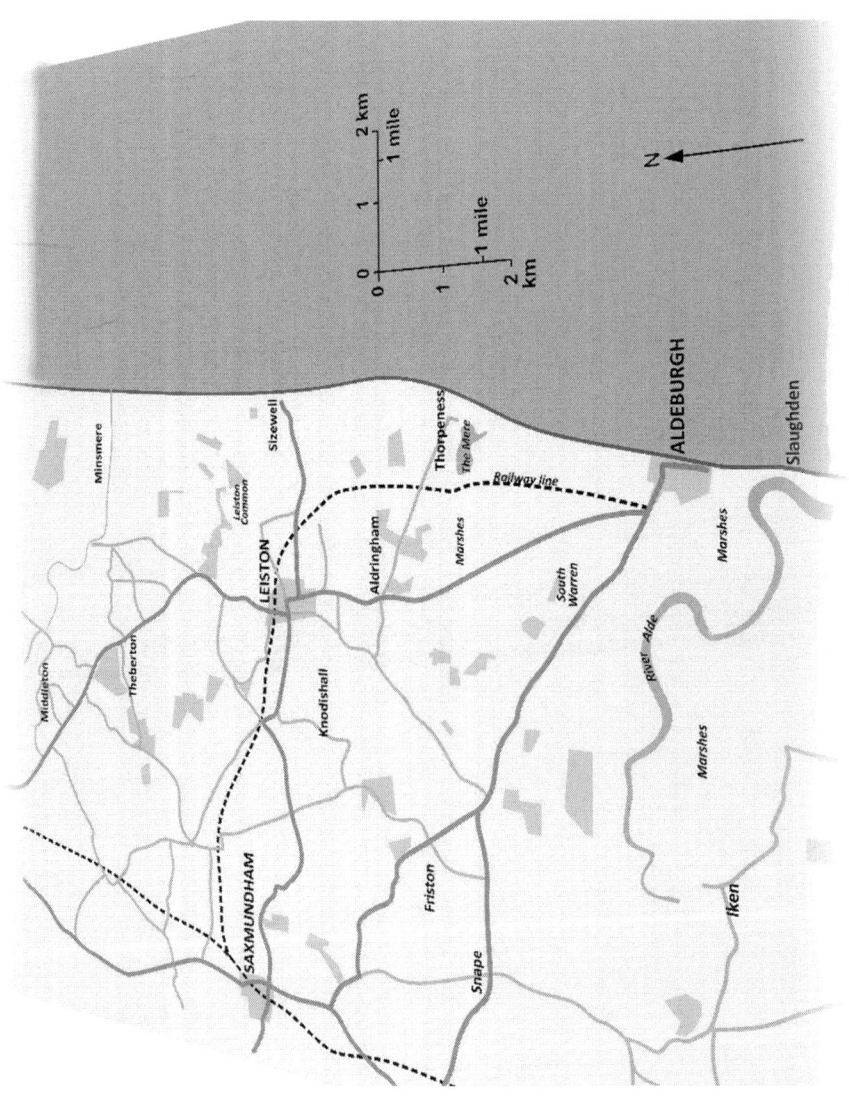

# APPENDIX 3

## Sketch-map showing features of the town of Leiston and locations of houses occupied by HCR

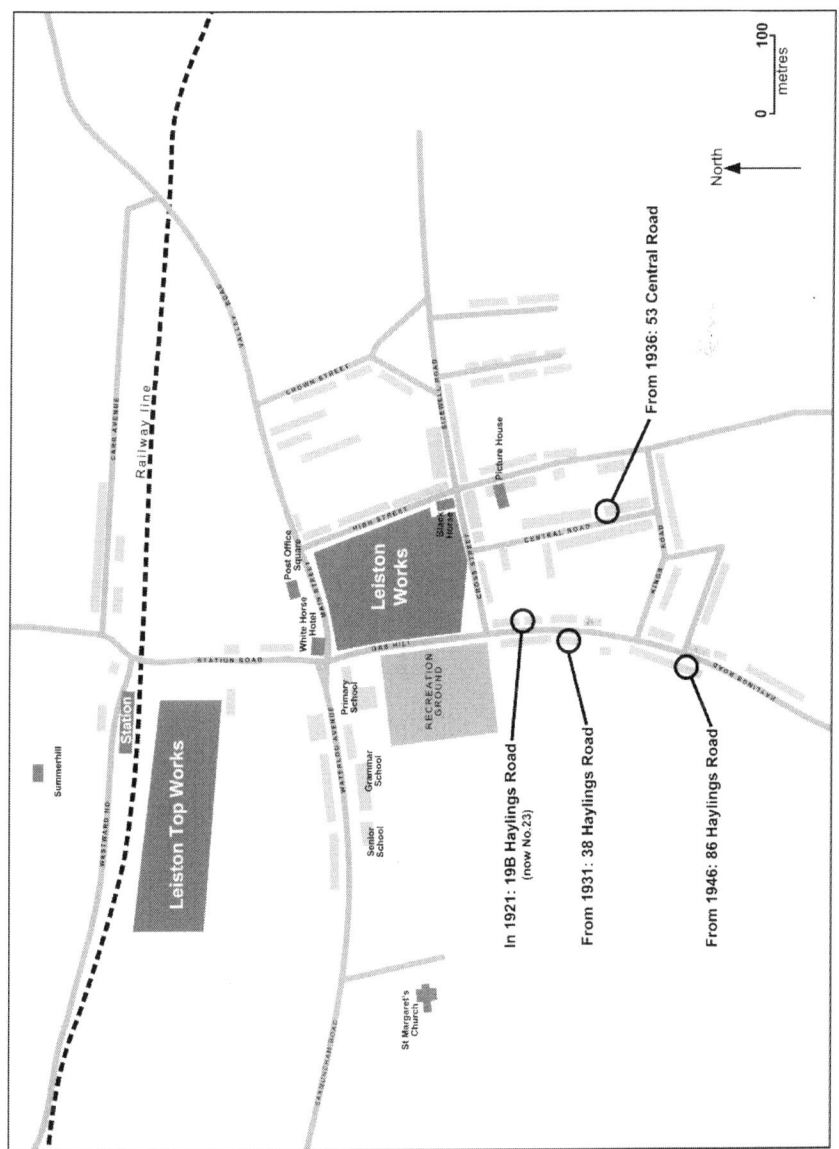

# APPENDIX 4

## Extracts from HCR's log book for April and October 1942

**N⁰ 97 SQUADRON    TATTERSHALL THORPE.**
**APRIL 1942.**

| Date | Hour | Aircraft Type and No. | Pilot | Duty | Remarks (Including results of bombing, gunnery, exercises, etc.) | Day | Night |
|---|---|---|---|---|---|---|---|
| | | | | | Time carried forward :— | 71·05 | 44·10 |
| 4/4/42 | 19.20 | Lancaster 5513(¹) | F/O MALTBY | Front Gunner. | N/F Cross Country. | | ·30 |
| 6/4/42 | 13.10 | Lancaster L7571(²) | F/O MALTBY | W/T. | Cross Country | ·40 | |
| 8/4/42 | 14.40 | Lancaster R5497(²) | F/O MALTBY | Front Gunner | N.F.T. | ·30 | |
| 8/4/42 | 21.15 | Lancaster R5495(³) | F/O MALTBY. | Front Gunner. | Operations - Gardening - Heligoland. | | 4.25 |
| 10/4/42 | 15.30 | Lancaster R5497(²) | F/O MALTAY. | W/T. | N.F.T. and Local. | ·25 | |
| 16/4/42 | 17.55 | Lancaster R5495(⁴) | F/O MALTBY. | Front Gunner. | E & A.F | ·25 | |
| 18/4/42 | 15.30 | Lancaster R5495(⁴) | F/O MALTBY. | Front Gunner. | N.F.T. | ·10 | |
| 18/4/42 | 20.55 | Lancaster R5495(⁴) | F/O MALTBY | Front Gunner | Base - Hexham - Base | | 2.00 |
| 21/4/42 | 16.00 | Lancaster R5497(⁵) | F/O MALTBY. | Front Gunner. | 4000' Bombing Wainfleet. | ·50 | |
| 22/4/42 | 13.25 | Lancaster R5495(⁴) | F/O MALTBY | Front Gunner | N.F.T. | ·20 | |
| 23/4/42 | 13.20 | Lancaster R5495(⁴) | F/O MALTBY | Front Gunner | Base - Lossiemouth | 2.40 | |
| 27/4/42 | 20.15 | Lancaster R5495(⁴) | F/O MALTBY | Front Gunner | Operations - Trondheim - Von Tirpitz. 1- 4000 4- 500 | | 8·15 |
| 28/4/42 | 20.25 | Lancaster R5495(⁴) | F/O MALTBY | Front Gunner. | Operations - Trondheim - Von Tirpitz. 1- 4000 4- 500 | | 8·05 |
| 29/4/42 | 15.10 | Lancaster R5495(⁴) | F/O MALTAY | Front Gunner | Lossiemouth - Base. | 2.20 | |
| 30/4/42 | 14.50 | Lancaster R5487(V) | F/O MALTBY | Front Gunner | N.F.T. | ·25 | |
| | | | | | TOTAL FLYING HOURS FOR APRIL 1942. | 8 ·45 | 23 ·15 |
| | | | | | GRAND TOTAL. | | 23·00 |
| | | | | | | Total Time … 79·50 | 67·25 |

Signed ........ S/LDR.
FOR. O.C. 97 SQUADRON

Time carried forward :-   102.20  |  152.50

| Date | Hour | Aircraft Type and No. | Pilot | Duty | Remarks (including results on bombing, gunnery, exercises, etc.) | Flying Times Day | Night |
|---|---|---|---|---|---|---|---|
| 1/10/42 | 14.55 | LANCASTER R.5607 | (4) P/O. LANCEY. | W/T. | AIR FIRING. | 1·30 | — |
| 3/10/42 | 11·00 | LANCASTER R.5609 | (3) P/O. LANCEY. | W/T. | AIR FIRING. | 1·15 | 3½ |
| 3/10/42 | 15·00 | LANCASTER R.5701 | (4) P/O. LANCEY. | W/T. | N.F.T. | ·20 | ·45 |
| 3/10/42 | 19.25 | LANCASTER R.5701 | (4) P/O. LANCEY. | W/T. | OPERATIONS- KREFELD.  1·2000  D.S.B.C.  8×30 | | 4·10 |
| 3/10/42 | 14.25 | LANCASTER R.5701 | (4) P/O. LANCEY. | W/T. | TOPCLIFFE - BASE. | ·50 | |
| 5/10/42 | 14·30 | LANCASTER L.7577 | (2) P/O. LANCEY. | W/T. | N.F.T. | ·25 | |
| 6/10/42 | 19.35 | LANCASTER W.4175 | (4) P/O. LANCEY. | W/T. | OPERATIONS- OSNABRUCK. (BOOMERANG. ELEC. FAILURE) | | ·50 |
| 9/10/42 | 11.20 | LANCASTER R.5609 | (3) P/O. LANCEY. | W/T. | LOW-LEVEL FORMATION. | 1·40 | ½ |
| 10/10/42 | 12·00 | LANCASTER R.5609 | (3) P/O. LANCEY. | W/T. | LOW-LEVEL FORMATION. | 4·45 | |
| 11/10/42 | 11·40 | LANCASTER R.5609 | (3) P/O. LANCEY. | W/T. | LOW-LEVEL FORMATION. | 4·55 | ½ |
| 13/10/42 | 17·55 | LANCASTER W.4255 | (D) P/O. LANCEY. | W/T. | OPERATIONS- WISMAR.  1·4000.  D.S.B.C.  8×30 | | 6·30 |
| 13/10/42 | 18·50 | LANCASTER W.4255 | (D) P/O. LANCEY | W/T. | OPERATIONS- KIEL -  1·4000.  D.S.B.C.   8×30 | | 5·50 |
| 15/10/42 | 14·65 | LANCASTER W.4175 | (4) P/O. LANCEY | W/T. | N.F.T. | ·25 | |
| 16/10/42 | 14.45 | LANCASTER W.4255 | (D) P/O. LANCEY. | W/T. | LOW-LEVEL FORMATION. | 2·50 | |
| 17/10/42 | 11.55 | LANCASTER W.4255 | (D) P/O. LANCEY. | W/T. | OPERATIONS- LE CREUSOT - (BOOMERANG) | 2·15 | |
| 22/10/42 | 17·15 | LANCASTER L.7574 | (4) P/O. LANCEY. | W/T. | OPERATIONS- GENOA - (BOOMERANG. P.O. 4/E.) | | 2·05 |

TOTAL FLYING TIMES FOR OCTOBER 1942     21·1·103·06

GRAND TOTAL                                44·15

TOTAL TIME ...123·30   175·55

.................. W/CDR.
O.C.  97  SQUADRON.

.................... 3/LDR.
O.C.  "B" FLIGHT.

# APPENDIX 5

## Table showing individual aircraft flown in by Harold Rouse during 1942, and their final fates

| Type | Number (squadron code) | Dates HCR flew in aircraft (HCR raid number in bold) | Ultimate fate of aircraft where known |
|---|---|---|---|
| Manchester | L7463 (OF-P) | 10.01.42 | Caught fire and crashed in Denmark 24.02.42 |
| Manchester | L7474 (OF-Z) | 03-08.01.42 | Crashed at Horncastle 12.03.42 |
| Manchester | L7489 (OF-T) | 10-20.01.42 **(1)** | Abandoned/crashed in Denmark 09.05.42 |
| Lancaster | L7571 (OF-X) | 06.04.42, 07.05.42 **(6)** | Shot down over Germany 17.09.42 |
| Lancaster | L7574 (OF-N) | 20.02.42, 25.09.42, 22.10.42 **(22)** | Shot down over Berlin 23.11.42 |
| Lancaster | L7577 (OF-T) | 28.02.42, 23-25.08.42, 05.10.42 | In use as static trainer 02.07.43 |
| Lancaster | R5486 (OF-P) | 09-10.03.42 | Crashed at Finningley 23.03.42 |
| Lancaster | R5487 (OF-V) | 30.04.42-28.05.42 **(7) (8) (9) (10) (11)** | Shot down over Hamburg 26.07.42 |
| Lancaster | R5495 (OF-N) | 08-29.04.42 **(2) (3) (4)** | Shot down at Essen 09.06.42 |
| Lancaster | R5497 (OF-Z) | 10-21.04.42, 28.08.42, 08.09.42, 28.11.42 **(13) (14) (26)** | Shot down at Neustadt 17.12.42 |
| Lancaster | R5513 (OF-P) | 04.04.42 | Shot down at Augsburg 17.04.42 |
| Lancaster | R5552 (OF-P) | 06.05.42, 27.08.42 **(12)** | Crashed at Zuid Holland 21.12.43 |
| Lancaster | R5553 (OF-S) | 04-05.05.42 **(5)** | Crashed at Conings by 05.05.42 |
| Lancaster | R5559 (OF-W) | 22.08.42 | Not known |
| Lancaster | R5569 (OF-B) | 13.09.42 | Crashed at Scampton 14.11.42 |
| Lancaster | R5607 (OF-X) | 27.08.42, 01.10.42 | Shot down over Dorsten 13.03.43 |
| Lancaster | R5609 (OF-S) | 29.09.42-11.10.42 | In use for training 15.04.44 |
| Lancaster | R5631 (OF-unknown) | 01.08.42 | Still flying 04.06.44 |
| Lancaster | R5701 (OF-Y) | 10.09.42, 02.10.42 **(17)** | Shot down over Limburg 05.10.42 |
| Lancaster | R5738 (OF-D) | 23.09.42 **(16)** | Shot down over Limburg 10.01.43 |
| Lancaster | R5866 (OF-U) | 10-12.09.42 **(15)** | Crash landed 01.01.43, damaged on ground 25.09.44 |
| Lancaster | R5889 (OF-V) | 06.11.42-08.12.42 **(23) (24) (25) (27) (28)** | Damaged 08.03.43, crashed 09.07.43 |
| Lancaster | R5895 (OF-unknown) | 07-15.08.42 | Shot down over Berlin 22.01.44 |
| Lancaster | R5906 (OF-unknown) | 14-20.08.42 | Sold for scrap 22.05.47 |
| Lancaster | W4127 (OF-unknown) | 18.08.42 | Shot down over France 21.04.44 |
| Lancaster | W4175 (OF-U) | 06.10.42 **(18)** | Crashed at Conings by 30.03.43 |
| Lancaster | W4255 (OF-V) | 12-17.10.42 **(19) (20) (21)** | Crashed 12.12.42 |

Sources:
HCR logbook
http://www.sonsofdamien.co.uk/Man-Lanc%20serials%20page%204.htm
http://www.rafcommands.com/database/serials/
https://aviation-safety.net/wikibase/172579
https://internationalbcc.co.uk/history-archive/losses-database/

# APPENDIX 6

## Map showing main UK locations mentioned in this book

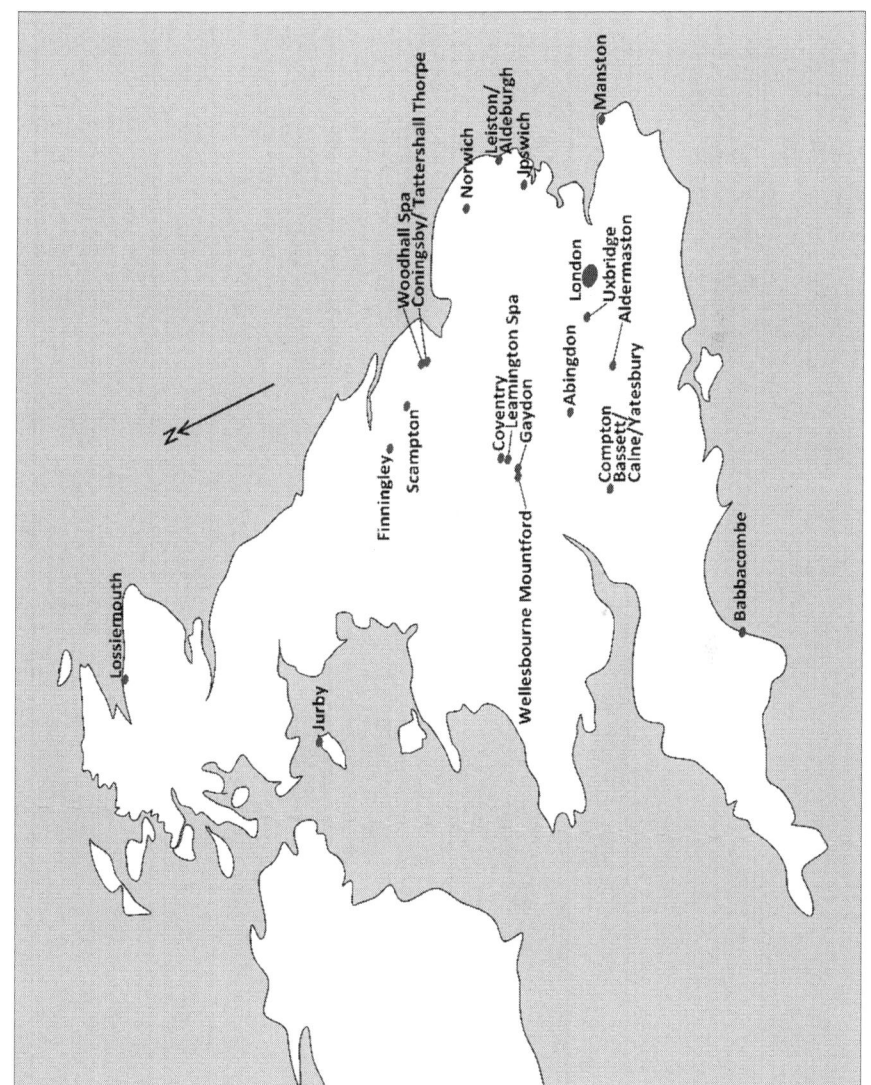

# APPENDIX 7

## Map showing combat operations flown by HCR during 1942

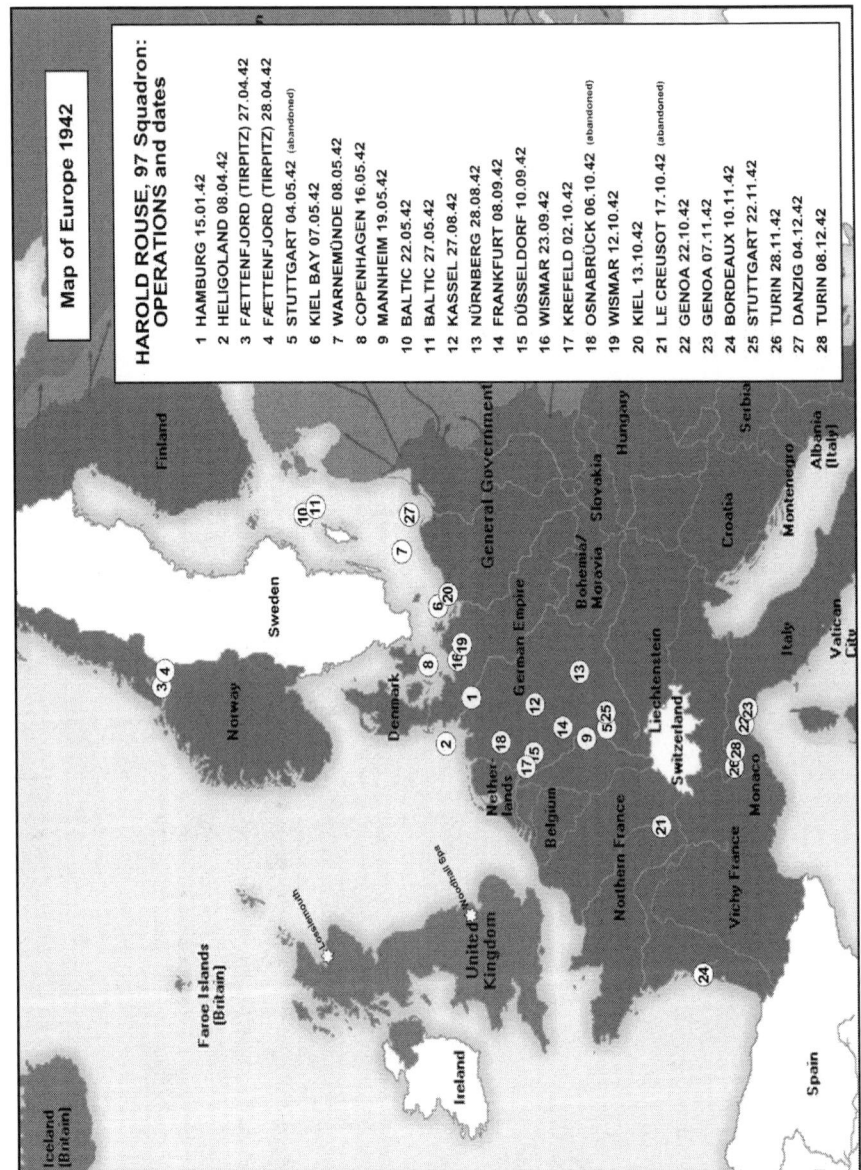

Map of Europe 1942

**HAROLD ROUSE, 97 Squadron: OPERATIONS and dates**

1 HAMBURG 15.01.42
2 HELIGOLAND 08.04.42
3 FÆTTENFJORD (TIRPITZ) 27.04.42
4 FÆTTENFJORD (TIRPITZ) 28.04.42
5 STUTTGART 04.05.42 (abandoned)
6 KIEL BAY 07.05.42
7 WARNEMÜNDE 08.05.42
8 COPENHAGEN 16.05.42
9 MANNHEIM 19.05.42
10 BALTIC 22.05.42
11 BALTIC 27.05.42
12 KASSEL 27.08.42
13 NÜRNBERG 28.08.42
14 FRANKFURT 08.09.42
15 DÜSSELDORF 10.09.42
16 WISMAR 23.09.42
17 KREFELD 02.10.42
18 OSNABRÜCK 06.10.42 (abandoned)
19 WISMAR 12.10.42
20 KIEL 13.10.42
21 LE CREUSOT 17.10.42 (abandoned)
22 GENOA 22.10.42
23 GENOA 07.11.42
24 BORDEAUX 10.11.42
25 STUTTGART 22.11.42
26 TURIN 28.11.42
27 DANZIG 04.12.42
28 TURIN 08.12.42

# INDEX

Page numbers shown in **bold** indicate those including relevant illustrations